美国语文

— ★ 家门外的大世界 ★ —

3

[美] 埃德温·埃尔德曼 ◎ 主编
朱生豪　等 ◎ 译

苏州新闻出版集团
古吴轩出版社

图书在版编目（CIP）数据

美国语文.家门外的大世界/(美)埃德温·埃尔德曼主编；朱生豪等译. -- 苏州：古吴轩出版社，2016.12（2024.9重印）
ISBN 978-7-5546-0814-2

Ⅰ.①美… Ⅱ.①埃… ②朱… Ⅲ.①英语课—小学—美国—教材 Ⅳ.①G624.311

中国版本图书馆CIP数据核字(2016)第277975号

责任编辑：蒋丽华
见习编辑：薛　芳
策　　划：党霄羽
封面设计：沈加坤

书　　名：美国语文——家门外的大世界
主　　编：[美]埃德温·埃尔德曼
译　　者：朱生豪　等
出版发行：苏州新闻出版集团
　　　　　古吴轩出版社
　　　　　地址：苏州市八达街118号苏州新闻大厦30F
　　　　　电话：0512-65233679　　邮编：215123
出 版 人：王乐飞
印　　刷：天津旭非印刷有限公司
开　　本：690mm×980mm　1/16
印　　张：18
版　　次：2016年12月第1版
印　　次：2024年9月第2次印刷
书　　号：ISBN 978-7-5546-0814-2
定　　价：49.80元

如有印装质量问题，请与印刷厂联系。022-22520876

推荐序一

李江月

（伊利诺斯大学PHD，湖北省高考作文满分获得者）

我在美国留学的时候，不仅要承担繁重的学习任务，还要传道授业，帮自己的导师们带本科新生。那时候我就经常想，要是有一套全新的教材，难度适中，学生和教师都能在书中获得营养，让来自中国的学生既能学习原汁原味的地道的美式英语，又能对自己所学的专业有所帮助，还能和各个领域的大咖们谈笑风生，打破很多美国人觉得中国人就是书呆子的刻板印象，那该多好啊！

这部千呼万唤始出来的《美国语文》丛书，解决了大家英语学习和教学的需求。每一篇课文都有精美的翻译，译文都做到了信达雅，读起来让人感觉如沐春风，甚至有时候让人感动，让学习英语这个看上去很繁重很枯燥的历程充满了惊喜。

众所周知，英语是不断变化的语言，也许需要每个学习者终身不断地学习。本套书的英文原版，是由常青藤名校校长精编精选，汇集了许多名家的经典之作，所以我们每一位读者，不仅是学生，还包括老师和家长，都能在这样美妙的阅读中感受到自己的进步，得到切切实实的满足感。这些美丽的体验，是市面上一般读物难以给予我们的。

相比很多所谓"高屋建瓴"的语言学著作，这部丛书经历了实践的考验，是一部非常亲民和接地气的青少年读物，也是家长和老师很好的帮手。

很多时候，因为应试教育的需求，同学们不得不死记硬背许多文学大家的作品，但是他们并不理解这些作品。于是，虽然短期内成绩提高了，却在成年后丧失了对文学的爱好和学习的欲望。不论在中国还是美国，总能看到这样令人遗憾的现象。对此，我们觉得很可惜，学习文学本来应该是一种乐趣，而不应该是一种负担。我们希望孩子们开心地学，家长们愉快地陪伴他们学习，老师们欣喜地发现孩子们的进步，而不是扼杀他们的兴趣，阻碍他们进一步追求知识的脚步。

我们知道，很多文学大师虽然不是专门的儿童作家，但是他们并不是没有给孩子写过作品。本套书的一大亮点就是集结了很多大家笔下从未被翻译成汉语的遗珠之作——在各领域专门为孩子创作的作品。通过阅读本套书，孩子们能在书中了解到许多新奇的知识，坐在家里就环游世界，也为未来的学习打下扎实的基础。

本书主编埃德温·埃尔德曼先生，用他的智慧和孜孜不倦的努力，代替了我们在文山书海的盲目搜寻，就像我们的另一双眼睛，带我们遨游浩瀚的书海，获取人类文明的精华。

一言以蔽之，这套丛书是我用过的最好的美国语文学习、教学的教材，既可以用来自学，也可以用到课堂上。特此，我将这部丛书诚挚推荐给大家。让我们一起在《美国语文》的海洋里自由地冲浪吧！

推荐序二

曹海元

（MIT PHD）

迄今为止，阅读一直是我最大的爱好，而在现今残存的记忆里，我最早读到可以真正称得上书的，正是父亲给我的那套页面泛黄的《上下五千年》。我在脑海里至今仍旧清晰地记得那套书的封面，茕茕孑立的烽火台，赭红的城楼，残阳如血。华夏五千年那时而诡谲绵密时而波澜壮阔的历史也随着作者娓娓道来的小故事，奔涌到我充满好奇的内心，溅起了一片片波澜。虽然以我当时的阅历和见识无法理解许多深奥的名词和藏在历史故事背后深刻的道理，但是那套书唤起了我内心对于知识的渴望。阅读让我得以坐上时光机，身临其境般在华夏文明的浩瀚长河中自由穿梭，在我的心中种下了星星之火。正是这些星星点点的火种，照亮了我内心通往知识殿堂的道路，让阅读成了我生命中最大的乐趣，从而造就了我今天这副模样。

《上下五千年》那套书在我如今看来，也许简陋不堪，只是一些历史小故事汇编，但在当年那个懵懂少年看来却已然是通往圣杯的指路明灯。如今这套《美国语文》无论从文章的文学艺术性、选材的宽泛多样性来说，还是从编排的科学合理性上来看，都要遥遥领先。阅读这套书的少年从中可以先领略中世纪灿若星河的文艺复兴，再遇见近现代疾风怒涛般的工业革命；可以先认识一生锋芒毕露最后却功亏一篑的拿破仑，再偶遇始终沉默寡言却在危难之际挽大厦于将倾的华盛顿。从弗吉尼亚的崎岖山岭到欧亚大陆的广袤平原，短短千言却包罗万象、荟萃乾坤，包含了世界历史、地理、博物、人物、传奇、诗歌等领域的精华。

在我看来，如果说《上下五千年》只是星星点点的火苗，那么这套《美国语文》则是那光芒四射的火炬。我想读者尤其是那些处于学习阶段的青少年，必然可以像当年的我那样，从这套书中找到点燃自己心中火种的火焰，照亮通往圣杯的道路。

最后，用我最爱的诗歌《伊萨卡岛》中的一句话来结尾——"当你启程，前往伊萨卡岛时，愿你的道路漫长，充满奇迹，充满发现。"这也是我对所有有幸读到这套丛书的读者的祝福。我想说的就这么多了，希望我无知和浅薄的序言不会让这套书的光芒逊色。

Preface

The classics presented in this volume have been selected from the standard literature of today and carefully arranged and graded to meet the mental development of pupils. In making these selections, great care has been taken to choose only those which are in themselves bright and attractive, and upon subjects of interest to children. Equal care has been taken to use only such as are written in words that come within the child's vocabulary and in a simple style, with no involved thought or difficult sentence structure. These selections may be classified as follows:

Legends
History and Biography
Fairy Tales
Story and Adventure
Stories of Animal Life
Poems of the Seasons
Miscellaneous Poems
Descriptions of People and Homes of Other Lands

This reader is based upon the vocabulary of the two books of the series which precede it. New words not found in the vocabularies of those two books are placed in word lists at the head of the chapter where they first occur. In schools where reading is taught either by the word or the sentence method, this arrangement is necessary. In schools where the phonic method has been used, it is equally valuable, because a previous study of the new word gives him that confidence without which no child can read with expression.

It is desirable, therefore, not only that real literature should be given him, but that the name and a few facts about the author should be associated with each selection. For this reason, a brief, interesting note about the author and his works will be found at the close of each selection. These biographical sketches are written in the vocabulary of this book and are to be studied by the class. In addition to the selections given, other stories or poems by the same author, suitable for reading by pupils, are suggested.

At frequent intervals through the volume, language lessons are given which furnish a systematic language drill, without any attempt whatever to teach technical grammar. The suggestions of each language lesson should not be limited in application to the story under which it is found, but should be judiciously used by teachers as an exercise with other reading lessons.

Grateful acknowledgment is made to publishers whose kindness has permitted us to use copyrighted material. In most instances special acknowledgments are made in connection with the selection and in the biographical sketch of the author. Among those not included in this way are: "Thinking Only of Myself", by Hezekiah Butterworth, published by Dana Estes and Company; "To Thomas Archer", by Robert Louis Stevenson, and "Moto's Elephant Hunt" by Henry M. Stanley, both published by Charles Scribners Sons, and "School in the Philippine Islands", by Adeline Knapp, published by Silver, Burdett and Company.

◈ 译文

前 言

　　本书中的经典篇目选自现当代的文学杰作，所有文章均经过精心编排和分级，符合学生心灵发展的规律。在收录过程中，我们侧重挑选基调明快、有吸引力的文章，所选作品的主题都是孩子们感兴趣的。另外，我们同样重视文章的语言和用词，比如本册选文中运用的词汇都是孩子们常用的，语言风格简单明了。所选篇目没有复杂的观点，也不采用难以理解的句式结构。本书所选篇目大致可分为以下几类：

传奇

历史与自传

童话故事

历险故事

动物的生活

咏叹四季

杂诗

异域生活

　　本书读者应具备本系列书第一、二册的词汇基础。当本册中首次出现前两册图书中未学过的新单词，将以列表形式呈现在每章的开头。学校的阅读教学通常从教授单词或分析句子入手，所以单词表十分重要。在学校的阅读教学中，还常常使用发音法，这种方法也同样重要，因为预习过新单词的学生能更加自信且富有感情地朗读课文。

　　我们希望学生们能通过每一篇文章接触真正的文学，同时也能对作者有一些了解，包括作者的名字以及其他信息。所以，我们在每篇文章的末尾都会对作者进行简短有趣的介绍。作者简介会保持本书一贯的语言风格，学生们可以在课堂上学到有关作者的知识。除了本书收录的选篇外，我们还推荐了每位作者创作的其他适合学生阅读的小说或诗歌。

  在本书中，每隔几篇选文会插一节语言课。语言课旨在提供系统的语言练习，但它不是专门的语法教学。建议教师在每节语言课上，不需要局限于课程下面的练习题，还可以选择其他文章，自行安排练习内容。

  最后要向出版商表示深深的感谢，他们善意地给我们提供了读物的版权。我们要特别感谢那些为本书内容以及作者简介做出贡献的人。除此之外，我们也感谢以其他方式支持本书的单位。他们是：达纳·埃斯蒂斯公司，他们提供了希西家·巴特沃斯的作品《怎能只想着自己》；查尔斯·斯克里布纳家族出版公司，他们提供了罗伯特·路易斯·斯蒂文森的《致托马斯·阿切尔的一封信》和亨利·莫顿·斯坦利的《莫托的大象狩猎之旅》；西尔弗·伯德特公司，他们提供了艾德林·纳普的《菲律宾群岛上的学校》。

目 录

Chapter 1　Descriptions of People and Homes of Other Lands ｜ 异域生活 001

Children in Japan ｜ 日本的孩子 003
A Visit to Venice ｜ 威尼斯之旅 006
To Thomas Archer ｜ 致托马斯·阿切尔的一封信 009
Foreign Children ｜ 外国小朋友 013
School in the Philippine Islands ｜ 菲律宾群岛上的学校 015
The Bazaars of Cairo ｜ 开罗的集市 018
Children in Turkey ｜ 土耳其的孩子们 021
A Letter From India ｜ 印度来的一封信 025
Chinese Children and Their Games ｜ 中国孩子和他们的游戏 ..028
The Education of a Young Prince ｜ 年轻王子的教育 032

Chapter 2　Legends&Story and Adventure ｜ 传奇和历险故事 037

King Arthur and the Sword Excalibur ｜ 亚瑟王和神剑 039
Sir Galahad and the Round Table ｜ 加哈拉德与圆桌骑士 042
The Holy Grail ｜ 圣杯 045
Daniel ｜ 但以理 046
Trout Fishing ｜ 钓鱼历险记 050
Thinking Only of Myself ｜ 怎能只想着自己 053

Chapter 3 Poems of the Seasons ｜ 咏叹四季 059

Under the Greenwood Tree ｜ 绿树荫下 061

Crocuses ｜ 番红花 064

Goldenrod ｜ 黄花 065

Autumn ｜ 秋 067

The Story of a Seed ｜ 种子的故事 070

March ｜ 进行曲 073

The Voice of Spring ｜ 春之声 075

Ho! For the Bending Sheaves ｜ 噢! 压弯的庄稼捆 078

Chapter 4 Stories of Animal Life ｜ 动物的生活 081

Little Mitchell ｜ 小松鼠米切尔 083

The Envious Wren ｜ 妒忌的鹪鹩 088

Catching Charlie ｜ 捉住查理 091

Arnaux, Homing Pigeon ｜ 信鸽阿诺斯 094

Moti Guj(1) ｜ 莫蒂·古吉拉特（1）......098

Moti Guj(2) ｜ 莫蒂·古吉拉特（2）......102

The White Seal ｜ 白色小海豹 106

The Whale's Story ｜ 鲸鱼的故事 111

Chspter 5 Fairy Tales ｜ 童话故事 115

Quackalina ｜ 鸭妈妈丽娜 117

The Image and the Treasure ｜ 雕像与财宝 121

Little Carl's Christmas ｜ 小卡尔的圣诞节 124

The Day Brothers ｜ 星期的故事 130

The Pony Engine | 小火车头的故事 133
The Swiss Clock's Story | 瑞士钟的故事 138
The New Year Came of Age | 新年的成人礼 143
The Three Wishes | 三个愿望 147

Chapter 6　Miscellaneous Poems | 杂诗 151

Hiawatha's Sailing | 海华沙的航行 153
A Close Race | 紧追不舍的赛跑 162
The Corn Song | 玉米之歌 165
Sweet and Low | 轻轻地，柔柔地 167
The Dream of the Boys | 男孩们的梦 169
Over the Hill | 山的那一边 172
Today | 今日 175
The Barefoot Boy | 赤脚的男孩 177
A Simple Recipe | 简单的窍门 181
The Miller of the Dee | 迪河边的磨坊主 183
Only One Mother | 只有一位大地之母 186
What the Wood-Fire Said | 柴火说了什么 187
Ring Out, Wild Bells | 响吧，狂野的钟 192
My Country, 'tis of Thee | 祖国之歌 193
The Rock-a-by Lady | 摇篮夫人 196
The Gladness of Nature | 大自然的喜悦 199
Whippoorwill Song | 夜鹰之歌 202
The Prayeth Best | 最好的祷告 204
Selection | 选段 205

Bob White | 一只叫鲍勃·怀特的鹑鸟 206

The Toadstool | 毒蘑菇 208

Chater 7　History and Biography | 历史与自传 209

The Young Surveyor | 年轻的测量员 211

Doing His Best | 尽己所能 217

The Return of Columbus to Spain | 哥伦布返航西班牙 220

Columbus | 哥伦布 223

Sir Walter Scott's Dogs | 沃尔特·司各特爵士的狗 224

The Boy That Was Hired Out | 租来的男孩 227

A Southern Officer to His Boys | 一名南部军官写给儿子们的信 232

Cadet Grant at West Point | 尤里西斯在西点军校 236

Chief John Marshall | 大法官马歇尔 241

Chapter 8　Stories of Kids | 儿童故事 245

Cotton(1) | 棉花（1）.. 247

Cotton(2) | 棉花（2）.. 251

Lilies and Cat-Tails(1) | 百合和香蒲(1) 254

Lilies and Cat-Tails(2) | 百合花和香蒲（2）.................................. 257

Jack and Tony's Friendship(1) | 杰克与托尼的友谊（1）............. 260

Jack and Tony's Friendship(2) | 杰克与托尼的友谊（2）............. 264

Rosetta Pope's School | 罗塞塔·蒲柏的学校 269

《美国语文》译者名录

Chapter 1

Descriptions of People and Homes of Other Lands | 异域生活

预习

bamboo /ˌbæmˈbuː/ 竹子
bead-like /ˈbiːdlˈaɪk/ 像珠子一样
during /ˈdʊrɪŋ/ 期间
holiday /ˈhɑːlədeɪ/ 节日
hopscotch /ˈhɑːpskɑːtʃ/ 跳房子
Japan /dʒəˈpæn/ 日本
kimono /kɪˈmoʊnoʊ/ 和服
manners /ˈmænəz/ 举止
movement /ˈmuːvmənt/ 动作
sleeves /sˈliːvz/ 袖子
temple /ˈtempl/ 寺庙
whether /ˈweðər/ 是否

Children in Japan

If you wish to see the children of Japan, let us take a little walk. We pass through a street shaded by cherry trees, and soon reach a temple. Here there are pretty grounds with many trees. The grounds are filled with children at play, and women talking.

The women carry their babies with them. Each little one is tied in a fold of his mother's loose coat, or gown, and carried on her back. In such places, babies are often seen in Japan.

If the mother is busy indoors, the baby is fastened on the back of an older brother or sister.

Sometimes this brother or sister is but little older than the baby. We shall see hundreds of children not more than five or six years of age, carrying, on their small shoulders, the baby of the house.

The baby is often fast asleep, and his tiny, smooth, brown head swings here and there with every movement of his small nurse.

The nurse walks, runs, sits, and jumps, flies kites, plays hopscotch, and fishes for frogs, never thinking whether the baby is sleeping or awake.

The little boys and girls of Japan are gentle in manners, and look very pretty in their wide sleeves and flowing kimonos. They have pretty feet and hands, and bead-like black eyes, which look at you without fear or shyness.

The children have their own holidays. The third day of the third month is the yearly holiday for all little girls. Then everyone buys toys for them that resemble things found in their homes.

The boys' great day falls on the fifth day of the fifth month. Then a tall bamboo pole rises from the door of every house where boys have been born in the past seven years.

At the top of the pole, huge fish of all colors, mostly purple and gold, float. There is one fish for each son in the family.

(Edwin Arnold)

译文

日本的孩子

如果你想要看看日本的孩子，让我们出去稍微走一走吧。穿过一条樱花树掩映的大街，不久就来到一处庙宇之前的庭院。这里风景优美，树木丰茂。这片空地上，到处都是嬉戏的孩子和闲谈的妇人。

妇人们是带着娃娃来的。每个小家伙都被绑在妈妈宽松的外衣里或者和服上，让妈妈背着。全日本的娃娃都在这样的环境中生活。

如果日本妈妈在家里忙活，娃娃就会被系在哥哥或姐姐的后背上。

有时候，哥哥或者姐姐只比小娃娃大一点儿。我们能见到数以百计的孩子，他们不过五六岁的年纪，小小的肩膀上背着自己家里的弟弟妹妹。

　　婴儿小小的、光滑的黄色脑袋，随着这些小保姆的走动摇来摇去，这样他就能迅速入睡。

　　而这些小小的保姆或走，或跑，或坐，或跳，或放风筝，或跳房子，又或者抓青蛙，从来都不考虑背上的婴儿是醒着还是睡着。

　　日本的小男孩和小女孩举止彬彬有礼，穿着宽袍大袖的和服，看起来非常可爱。他们的手脚都很美丽，眼睛像黑珠子一般。当他们看着你的时候，目光中既没有羞涩，也没有畏惧。

　　孩子们也有自己的假期。每年的三月三日，就是小女孩们的节日。在这一天，每个人都会给她们买过家家的玩具。

　　而对于男孩来说，五月五日是一个盛大的日子。男孩们满七岁之前，每一年的这一天，他出生的那所房子前都要竖起一根高高的竹竿。在竹竿的顶上是大大的彩色鱼旗，旗子的颜色常常是黄紫相间的。家里有一个男孩，就要有一面这样的鱼旗。

（埃德温·阿诺德）

◇ 作者介绍

　　1852年，埃德温·阿诺德爵士还是牛津大学的学生时，就赢得了"伯沙撒的盛宴"诗歌奖。他曾游历于印度、日本等东方各国，创作了大量相关作品。他最伟大的诗歌作品是《亚洲之光》。本文《日本的孩子》摘自于《日本植物》一书。该书由查尔斯·斯克里布纳家族出版公司在美国出版。

◇ 练习

1.用英文写出"三月份的第三天"。

_____

2.用英文写出"五月份的第五天"。

_____

A Visit to Venice

Venice, August 13, 1882.

Dear Gertie:

When the little children in Venice want to take a bath, they just go down to the front steps of the house and jump off, and swim around in the street.

Yesterday I saw a nurse sitting on the front steps, holding one end of a string, and the other end was tied to a little fellow, who was swimming down the street.

When he went too far, the nurse pulled in the string, and brought the baby home again.

Then I met another youngster, swimming in the street, whose mother had tied him by the side of the door. When he tried to swim away to see another boy, who was tied to another post down the street, he couldn't, and they had to call out to each other over the water.

Isn't this a queer city?

You are always in danger of running into some of the people and drowning them, for you go about in a boat instead of a carriage, and use an oar instead of a horse. But it is so pretty, and the people, especially the children, are very bright, and gay and handsome.

When you are sitting in your room at night, you hear some music under your window, and look out. There you see a boat in which are a man with a fiddle, and a woman with a voice, and they are serenading you.

To be sure, they want some money when they have finished, for everybody begs here, but they do it very prettily and are full of fun.

Tell Susie that I did not see the queen this time. She was out of town. But ever so many noblemen and princes have sent to know how Toody was doing, and how she looked, and I have sent them all her love.

There must be lots of pleasant things to do at Andover, and I think that you must have had a beautiful summer there.

Pretty soon now you will go back to Boston. Please do go into my house when you get there, and see if the doll and her baby are well and happy (but do not carry them off); and make the music box play a tune, and remember your affectionate uncle.

Philips

🕮 译文

威尼斯之旅

亲爱的格蒂：

　　你肯定想不到，当威尼斯的小孩子想要洗澡的时候，他们只要走下房子前面的台阶，"扑通"一声跳下去，然后就可以在"街"上游来游去了。

　　昨天我看见一位保姆坐在房前的阶梯下，手里抓着一根绳子，绳子的一头系着个小家伙。他正兴高采烈地在"街"上游泳呢！

　　每次他游远了，保姆就会往回拉绳子，小家伙又回到了家门前。

　　接着我遇见了另外一个在街上游泳的小孩子。母亲把他系在了门边上，他想要游得远一点去看另一个男孩，但做不到。那个男孩和他一样被系在街前方的另一根柱子上。他们毫无办法，只好在水面上叫着对方的名字。

　　这是不是一个很奇怪的城市？

　　出门的时候，你得摇摇晃晃地乘船，而不是安安稳稳地坐在车厢里；你得学会用桨划船，而不是驾马拉车；总是有可能会撞到什么人，弄不好会导致他溺水。不过，这儿确实非常漂亮，这里的人，特别是孩子，个个聪明英俊，幸福快乐。

　　晚上你坐在房间里的时候，会听见窗户下响起音乐声。从窗户看出去，你会看见一条小船。一个男人拉着小提琴，一个女人和着音乐歌唱，他们正在为你唱小夜曲。

　　当然，你得给他们赏点零钱。虽然这里每个人都会乞讨，但他们总能让这乞讨显得有趣优雅。

　　跟苏珊说，我这次没有看到王后，她不在城里。许多王公贵族寄信来问候托蒂，想知道她看起来怎么样，我已经寄了回信，替她表示感谢和爱意。

　　在安多弗肯定有许多愉快的事情值得去做。我想你一定能在那儿度过一个美妙的夏天。

很快你就要回波士顿了。记得到时候一定要到我的家里看看,看看洋娃娃和她的小宝宝是否一切都好(但不可以把她们抢走),你还可以转动音乐盒让它发出美妙的曲调。叔叔永远爱你!

菲利普

1882年8月13日,写于威尼斯

✎ 练习

1. 学习写信(1)

(1)这封信是在什么地方写的?
_____

(2)这封信是什么时候写的?
_____

2. 抄写

(1)Springfield, Massachusetts.

(2)July 2, 1906.
_____
_____

3. 按照书信格式改编下文

(1)At Albany, in New York, on the tenth of May, 1905.

(2)In Virginia, at Richmond, September 4, 1899.
_____
_____

4. 抄写

(1)Mr. James M. Hall　　_____

(2)36 State Street　　　　_____

(3)Chicago　　　　　　　_____

(4)Illinois　　　　　　　　_____

To Thomas Archer

Island of Tahiti, November, 1888.

Dear Tom:

This is a much better place for children than any I have hitherto seen in these seas. The girls, and sometimes the boys, play a very grand kind of hopscotch.

The boys play horses just as we do in Europe. They also have very good fun on stilts, trying to knock each other down, in which they do not often succeed.

The children of all ages go to church, and are allowed to do what they please, running about the aisles, rolling balls, stealing mamma's bonnet and sitting on it, and eventually fall asleep on the floor.

I forgot to say that the whips to play horse, and the balls to roll about the church naturally grow on trees. The whips are so good that I wanted to play horse myself; but no such luck! My hair is gray, and I am a great, big, ugly man. The balls are rather hard, but very light and quite round.

But what I really wanted to tell you was this: beside the tree top toys (Hush-a-by, toy shop, on the tree top!), I have seen some real made toys, the first observed in the South Seas. This was how. You are to think of a four-wheeled gig; one horse; in the front seat two Tahiti people, in their Sunday clothes, blue coat, white shirt, kilt of blue stuff with big white or yellow flowers, legs and feet bare; in the back seat me and my wife, who is a friend of yours. We have straw hats, for the sun is strong.

We drive between the sea and the mountains. The road is cut through a forest mostly of fruit trees. The very creepers are heavy with a great and delicious fruit, bigger than your head and far nicer.

Presently we came to a house in a pretty garden, quite by itself, very nicely kept, the doors and windows open, no one about, and no noise but that of the sea. It looked like a house in a fairy tale. Just beyond we had to ford a river, and there we saw the people.

In the mouth of the river, where it met the sea waves, the children were ducking and bathing and screaming together like a flock of birds: seven or eight little brown boys and girls as happy as the day was long; and on the banks of the stream beside them, real toys-toy ships, full rigged, with their sails set, though they were lying in the dust on their beam ends.

You may care to hear, Tom, about the children in these parts; their parents obey them; they do not obey their parents; and I am sorry to tell you (for I dare say you are already thinking the idea a good one) that it does not pay one halfpenny.

There are three ways of living, Tom: the real old-fashioned one, in which children had to find out how to please their dear papas, or their dear papas punish them severely. This style did very well, but is now out of fashion.

Then there is the style that is followed in Europe; in this, children have to behave pretty well, go to school, and so on, or their dear papas will know the reason why. This does fairly well.

Then there is the South Sea Island plan, which does not do one bit. The children beat their parents here; it does not make their parents any better; so do not try it.

Remember us all to all of you, and believe me, yours,

Robert Louis Stevenson

译文

致托马斯·阿切尔的一封信

亲爱的汤姆：

这里真是我迄今见过的海外最适合孩子们生活的地方了。女孩们会玩各种跳房子的游戏，有时候男孩子也会加入她们的游戏。

这里的男孩也像欧洲的男孩们一样，喜欢玩一种叫作"骑马"的游戏，大家蹦跳着要去撞倒对方，虽然经常徒劳无功，但却乐在其中。

孩子们不论年龄大小都要去教堂，他们在教堂里可以随心所欲：在过道里奔跑，追逐滚来滚去的球，偷拿妈妈的帽子当垫子坐，玩累了就躺在地上睡觉。

我忘了说一件事，孩子们把树枝当作骑马游戏用的鞭子，把树上结的种子当作球在教堂里滚来滚去。那些鞭子简直太棒了，我都忍不住想要玩一玩骑马游戏了。不幸的是，我头发花白，又老又丑，已经成了个大人。那些球全都又坚韧又轻巧，还圆溜溜的。

对了，我想跟你说，包括这些"树上结的玩具"在内（嘘！听我说，玩具店真的就在树顶上），我曾经还见过真正鬼斧神工的造物。这是我在南太平洋的一个新发现。情景是这样的，你不妨想象一下：一辆四轮马车上，两名身穿周日便服的塔希提人坐在前面，他们上身是白色衬衫加蓝色外套，下身是一条大白花或是大黄花的蓝底苏格兰短裙，光着腿赤着脚；我和我的妻子（她当然也是你的朋友）坐在后面，戴着大大的草帽来遮挡强烈的阳光。

我们驾车奔驰于大海和大山之间，从果树林里穿过。又大又香的果实沉甸甸地挂在攀援植物上。哈哈，这果子绝对比你的头要大，当然也比你的头更好吃！

不久，我们来到一座漂亮的房子那里，房子四周都是花园，非常安静，打理得也很好。我们会把门窗全都打开，周围没有一个人，没有一点喧嚣，只听见海浪轻轻拍打的声音。屋子仿佛置身于童话故事里。我们渡过一条小河，才能看得到人群。

就在这条小河与海洋相汇的河口，孩子们像小鸟一样嬉闹着，他们潜入水中，在河里洗澡，兴奋地尖叫。七八个棕色皮肤的小孩子终日玩耍，非常开心。河岸上，一群小孩子将玩具船驶向河面。这些玩具船像真正的船一样配上索具，扬帆起航，虽然最后它们终将葬身于河底的淤泥。

汤姆，可能你听说过，这里的孩子不听父母的，相反，他们的父母总是听他们的。我不得不遗憾地告诉你（我敢说你一定想听），事实并非如此。

这里有三种教育子女的办法：一种是很传统的方式，孩子们得学会取悦父亲，否则父亲会严厉地惩罚他们。这种方式很管用，不过现在已经过时了。

第二种方式在欧洲也很流行。孩子们得好好表现，要么上学，要么干其他的营生，否则父亲非得寻根究底不可。这种方式也很管用。

第三种方式就是这个南太平洋岛屿特有的了,可以说一点用都没有。这里的孩子打自己的父母,这种办法可没有让他们的父母变得更好。因此,你还是不要去尝试这种方法了。

记得代我们全家向你们全家问好!

罗伯特·路易斯·斯蒂文森
1888年11月,写于塔希提岛

作者介绍

罗伯特·路易斯·斯蒂文森是苏格兰人。他不顾身体孱弱,经常四处旅行,最后定居于太平洋上的塔希提岛。

斯蒂文森先生把孩提时的所思所感、所作所为都写在了《儿童诗园》这本书里。他还专门为孩子们写了《珍宝岛》和《黑箭》这两本书。

练习

学习写信(2)

1. 抄写

(1) Remember me to all of you.

—————————————

(2) Take the packs off his back.

—————————————

(3) Do not fear.

—————————————

2. 表达要求或者命令的句子叫祈使句。

思考祈使句的标志是什么?然后写一写带有 let, listen, give, go, bring, do, ask, write, study 的祈使句。

—————————————

Foreign Children

Little Indian, Sioux or Crow,
Little frosty Eskimo,
Little Turk or Japanese,
Oh! Don't you wish that you were me?

You have seen the scarlet trees
And the lions over the seas;
You have eaten ostrich eggs,
And turned the turtles off their legs.

Such a life is very fine,
But it's not so nice as mine;
You must often, as you trod,
Have wearied not to be abroad.

You have curious things to eat,
I am fed on proper meat;
You must dwell on beyond the foam,
But I am safe and live at home.

Little Indian, Sioux or Crow,
Little frosty Eskimo,
Little Turk or Japanese,
Oh! Don't you wish that you were me?

(Robert Louis Stevenson)

译文

外国小朋友

印第安小朋友，苏族克罗族小朋友，
满身是雪的因纽特小伙伴，
突厥或日本小伙伴，
噢！难道你们不企盼，成为我这样的小小孩？

你曾见过红树林，
目睹海外雄狮群；
尝过鸵鸟大圆蛋，
翻个乌龟底朝天。

你的生活诚然可贵，
怎及我的生活圆满；
当你迈开脚步，
一定想去国外看看。

你的食物稀奇古怪，
我的食物很是普通；
你住在漂着泡沫的海上，
我的家安安全全。

印第安小朋友，苏族克罗族小朋友，
满身是雪的因纽特小伙伴，
突厥或日本小伙伴，
噢！难道你们不企盼，成为我这样的小小孩？

（罗伯特·路易斯·斯蒂文森）

School in the Philippine Islands

As I was driving through the city of Manila one day, the coachman suddenly turned around and said, "Me study Americano(American)."

"What do you study?" I asked.

Proudly he drew from his pocket a soiled card. It was an old bill of fare from the leading American restaurant. Then he read aloud, pointing out each word: "Ham, potatoes, beefsteak, pork, beans, eggs, etc.," and stopped to receive the praise that he knew he deserved. He was asked why he did not go to school.

"No time. Must work."

"But you could go to night school," I said.

"No dinero(money)."

It was explained to him that the night school is free, but this was more than he could believe. Then another Filipino, who was a clerk, and who spoke English, explained it to him.

At last he understood the surprising fact, and his face glowed with pleasure. "Mucho buena!" he exclaimed; "mi vamos!" (Very good! I go!)

It is no wonder that the boy found it hard to believe the American schools free. There had never before been free schools in the islands. There were always pay schools, but the Spanish language was not taught. The children studied their own strange language.

Hundreds of these queer schools are still left. They are to be found in every village. Such a school is nearly always held in the hut of some village dame.

If we were to go into one of these schools, we should find a dozen or more boys and girls lying or sitting on the bamboo floor. They study their lessons at the top of their voices. They do not merely read aloud; they shout.

One little fellow, lying on his back, his feet waving in the air, his tongue rattling off his lesson at full speed and voice, can make a great deal of noise. It is the old story of the pig under a gate: ten such boys can make much more noise than one. So it is never hard to find the village school.

The teacher hears the lessons while she prepares the noonday "chow", or lunch, of rice and fish, or puts her house in order, or smokes her long brown cigar.

The only books that they have in these schools are little primers and readers, so the poor children learn very little.

But these children can learn quickly when they are well taught. It is wonderful to note their progress in English. One boy twelve years old, who had been studying English only four months, came to his American teacher one morning. He had in his hand a book that American boys like, "Ten Boys on the Road from Long Ago to Now."

"Three stories of these I have read, Teacher, and I enjoy them very much," he said. It is good to learn that the Filipino boys' hearts are so like our own.

(Adeline Knapp)

译文

菲律宾群岛上的学校

一天，我正坐车穿过马尼拉市区时，马车夫突然转过身来对我说："我，学，美国话。"

"你学了什么呢？"我问道。

他自豪地从口袋中摸出一张脏兮兮的卡片，那是一家知名美国餐馆很早以前的菜单，然后指着上头的单词一个接一个地大声读了起来："火腿、土豆、牛排、猪肉、豆子、鸡蛋……"随即停下来接受应得的称赞。我问他为什么不去上学。

"没有时间。必须工作。"

"但你可以去上夜校。"我说。

"没钱。"

我向他解释，夜校是免费的，但他全然不信。随后另一个会说英文的菲律宾职员向他解释了此事。

最终他明白了这个惊人的事实，脸上因为喜悦而泛出了红光。他用西班牙语大叫道："太好了！我去！"

这孩子不相信美国学校都是免费的也不足为奇。在这片岛屿群上，从来没有过免费学校。这里只有付费学校，而且也不教西班牙语。孩子们学习当地人自己的奇特语言。

数以百计奇特的学校留存至今，每个村庄中都有。课堂总是设在一些乡村妇女的小屋内。

如果我们走进一所此类学校，会发现十几个男孩女孩在竹地板上或躺或坐，用最大的嗓门来读课文。他们已经不只是在大声朗读了，简直是在吼叫。

一个仰面躺着、双脚在空中摆动，并以最快、最大声音背诵着课文的小孩子能制造巨大的噪音。正如两只猪"哼哼"的声音比一只猪要大，十个这样的男孩比一个吵得多。因此，凭着这样的噪音，找到一所乡村学校并不难。

老师"听"着课文的时候，用稻米鱼肉准备午餐，或者在收拾屋子，抽着长长的棕色雪茄。

这种学校只有几本入门读物，所以可怜的孩子们没多少东西可学。

但这些儿童只要受到了良好教育，就学得很快，他们在英文上的进步简直不可思议。一天早晨，一位才学了四个月英文的十二岁男孩来找他的美国老师，他手中拿着一本《从古至今的十个小男孩》。这本书美国男孩也喜欢看。

他说："老师，我读了其中的三个故事，都很喜欢。"得知这个菲律宾男孩和我们怀有同样的情感，真是一件令人欣慰的事情。

（艾德林·克纳普）

The Bazaars of Cairo

The Mooskee is the best known street in Cairo. It is also the only one in the old part of the town which the traveler can find without a guide. It runs straight for a mile, perhaps, and is broad enough for carriages.

A large part of this street is roofed with cane or palm slats. Through these the sun sifts a little light, and the street is cool and pleasant. No other street in the world seems to show so many kinds of people and in no other one can be heard so many languages.

If the Mooskee is crowded, the bazaars are a jam. Things that are wanted are far apart. If one wishes to make two or three purchases, he must use a whole day.

In one quarter are red slippers, nothing but red slippers, hundreds of shops hung with them; the yellow slippers are in another quarter, and by no chance does one merchant keep both kinds.

There are the silk bazaars, the gold bazaars, the silver bazaars, the brass, the arms, the cotton, the spice, and the fruit bazaars.

And what is a bazaar? Merely a lane, roofed with matting it may be, on each side of which are little shops, not much bigger than a dry-goods box. Often there is a story above, with hanging balconies and latticed windows.

On the ledge of his shop the merchant, in fine robes of silk and linen, sits cross-legged, perhaps smoking. He sits all day sipping coffee and talking with his friends. At the time of prayer, he spreads his prayer-carpet in public, and says his prayers.

On the other side of the street is a shop where three men sit cross-legged, making cashmere shawls by piecing old bits of Indian scarves.

On the next corner is a public fountain, and over it is heard the "studying" of a school. It is a boys' school, and both the master and the pupils are sitting on the floor.

Each pupil has before him his lesson written on a wooden tablet, and this he is reading at the top of his voice. He commits his lesson to memory, all the time swaying backwards and forwards.

With twenty boys shouting together, the noise is heard above all the sounds of the street. If a boy looks off or stops reciting, the stick of the schoolmaster sets him going again.

The boys learn first the alphabet, then the ninety-nine names of God. They next take up the Koran. This they learn chapter by chapter. If the boy needs writing and arithmetic, he learns them from the steelyard weigher in the market.

Sitting in the bazaar for an hour, one will see strange sights. We can never get used to the ungainly camel. He thrusts his huge bulk into the narrow lane, and stretches his snake neck from side to side.

His dark driver sits high up in the dusk of the roof on the wooden saddle, and sways to and fro with the long stride of the beast.

(Charles Dudley Warner)

译文

开罗的集市

摩色是开罗最有名的一条街，这也是老城区里唯一游客不需要向导就能找到的街。这条街大约有一千米多长，宽度足够一辆四轮马车通过。

这条街的大部分地方都种着藤类植物或是棕榈树，阳光从枝叶间洒下来，令人感到清凉愉快。世界上再没有哪条街像摩色这样人种众多了。在这里你能听到各种各样的语言。

摩色街拥挤的时候，两边的集市也挤满了人。人们需要的货物总是隔得很远，如果有人想要采购两三样货物，他得花上一整天的时间。

有一个区域专门卖红色的拖鞋——是的，只有红色拖鞋。许多小铺子上挂满了红色拖鞋。黄色的拖鞋在另一个区域出售，并且绝没有哪个商人同时出售这两种拖鞋。

摩色街上有丝绸集市、黄金集市、白银集市，还有黄铜、武器、棉花、香料和水果集市。

那么，集市到底是什么样子呢？其实不过是一条顶上搭着席子的小巷子，很多小店紧挨着排在两旁。这些店非常小，比纺织箱都大不了多少。通常人们会在露台和格子窗上挂一块记录着历史沿革的招牌。

一个商人穿着丝绸和亚麻制成的长袍，盘着腿坐在店铺边上，也许还抽着烟。他整天坐在那里，啜饮着咖啡，和朋友们侃侃而谈。到了祷告的时间，他就在大家面前铺开祷告毯，进行祷告。

街道另一边的小店里，三个男人盘腿而坐，利用印度围巾上拆下来的绒布片制作山羊绒披肩。

另一个街角里有一个公共水池，它的上空回荡着从学校传来的朗朗书声。那是一所男子学校，教师和学生都席地而坐。

每个学生前面都得放一块写着功课的木板，还得用最大的嗓门诵读，他得保证记住这些功课。学生们都前仰后合地读着这些木板。

二十个男孩一起大声叫喊的声音盖住了街上的其他动静。如果哪个男孩开了小差，或是停止了背诵，教师就会用教鞭提醒他，让他继续。

男孩们先是学习字母表，然后学习神的九十九种称呼。然后他们会一章接一章地学习《古兰经》。如果有男孩需要学习书写和算术，市场里用秤杆称重的人就可以教他。

在集市里坐上一个小时，你会看见许多奇妙的景象。笨拙的骆驼把它庞大的身躯强行塞进狭窄的小巷，蛇一样的脖子从这边伸到那边，摆个不停。这幅景象我们永远都没法适应。

黄昏，黑皮肤的赶驼人高高坐在木鞍上，骆驼每次大大地跨上一步，赶驼人就要来回摇摆一回。

（查尔斯·达德利·沃纳）

作者介绍

查尔斯·达德利·沃纳在马萨诸塞州和纽约州度过了少年时期，不过他人生的最后几年是在康涅狄格州度过的。沃纳先生把他的早年生活写在《做个男孩》一书中。这本书讲了一个非常轻松愉快的故事。

该作者还写了许多关于旅行的有趣的书。本文选自《尼罗河的冬天》一书，并获得了该书出版商霍顿·米夫林的授权。

Children in Turkey

The city of Constantinople is sometimes spoken of as "the dream-city come true". This is because we may yet find in this city so many of the wonderful things described in the "Arabian Nights".

Everywhere in the streets are open shops, or "booths", in which are sold the rich carpets, and rugs and stuffs of the East.

If you want to see the children of Constantinople on a holiday, you must visit the "Sweet Waters of Asia". This is a park not far from the great city.

Here you will see whole families with their servants and slaves, black and white. Children by the score play around the green under the plane trees.

Yellow corn on the cob, smoking hot, is sold by peddlers to the groups of families, who eat it off the ear. Candy and cakes in every shape are also sold, and all sorts of toys.

These children are very polite to strangers. The higher a person is in rank, the lower is the bow, or salaam, that is made to him. One little boy that saluted us touched the earth with his right hand, brought it up to his mouth, and then tipped his forehead.

This is a courtesy which, from a child, says: "From the earth, our mother, I give you my heart, and with my hand to my brow, I salute you!"

By the time the boy has reached his sixth year, he begins to think about school. His father and mother then give him small presents. Among these there is always a bag with a strap. This is to be hung on his shoulder.

The bag is square in shape, and is large enough to hold his primary book. Then the book is bought. The bag and the book are covered with embroidered work.

The day to begin school is decided upon. It is a day marked with the whitest stone. Word is sent to the teacher, and the other pupils are told of the great event.

Then a pony is bought, and fitted up with a handsome saddle and bridle. No such ponies as the spirited, yet gentle, iron-gray ponies of the East are to be found elsewhere in the world.

All the other pupils in the school come to the house of the new pupil. The little boy is placed on the pony, and all the other children form a double line in front.

Then the procession moves, the children singing a hymn. The little horse, with the little hero of the day, follows. The pony seems to feel very important.

The little girls in Turkey go to the same school as the boys. They wear a great many flowers and feathers. The boys and girls all study together.

A primary school has one or two rooms. Around three sides of each of the rooms there are large divans against the walls. The seat of the teacher is on the fourth side.

The pupils sit cross-legged in a line on the divans. They hold their books on their knees, and recite, all at the same time, in a loud, shrill voice.

After they are able to read a little from the Koran, they take up writing. As there are no writing tables or desks, they hold their copy-books in their hands.

They learn grammar, also, and the four rules of arithmetic.

This is all the education that they receive in the primary schools. Most of the people have to be satisfied with this. Wealthy men, however, hire teachers from other countries in Europe to assist their children in the study of languages.

(Samuel S. Cox)

☞ 译文

土耳其的孩子们

某种程度上说，君士坦丁堡是"梦想成真"的代名词，因为我们已经在这里发现了许多《一千零一夜》中描写的奇妙事物。

街上到处是开放式的商店，或者说是"售货棚"，里面出售昂贵的大地毯、小地毯以及充满东方风情的商品。

假日期间要想见到君士坦丁堡的儿童，你必须到一个叫作"亚洲甜水"的公园逛上一圈。它离城市中心不远。

在这里，你会看到许多带着仆人和奴隶——他们有黑人也有白人——的土耳其家庭。儿童们成群结队地在法国梧桐树下的草地上玩耍。

小贩们向这些家庭售卖冒着热气的黄澄澄的玉米棒，这些玉米棒烫得他们边吃边摸耳朵。小贩们还贩卖种类齐全的玩具和各种形状的糖果和蛋糕。

这些儿童对待陌生人很有礼貌。陌生人的身份越高，他们鞠躬时身体就压得越低。额手礼就是为这样的人创造的。一个向我们致意的小男孩用右手触地，接着轻触他的嘴巴，然后斜放在他的前额上。

孩子对你行这样的礼，意思是："在大地母亲的见证下，我把全副身心献给你，向你致意！"

男孩长到六岁的时候就该考虑去上学了。他的父母会送小礼物给他。这些礼物中总会有一只书包。书包上带有带子，方便他把书包挂在肩膀上。

书包是方形的，大小足够放得下他的小学课本。父母把这些课本买回家，把书包和课本都装饰起来。

开学的日子是早就定好了的，这是一个幸福的日子。教师得到消息之后，会把这件大事告知其他的学生。

接着父母会买一匹小马，装配好帅气的马鞍和缰绳。世界其他地方都找不到这种东方特有的铁灰色小马，它们精力充沛又温柔可亲。

学校里的其他学生来到屋子里欢迎新学生。小男孩骑在小马上，其他孩子在前面排成两行。

仪式继续进行，孩子们唱起赞美诗，在前引领小马和这天的小主角前行。小马看上去感觉非常威严。

土耳其的小女孩和男孩去同一所学校。她们用许多花和羽毛装饰自己，和男孩们在一起学习。

一所小学有一到两个房间。每一个房间都靠着三面墙放着巨大的矮沙发。第四面墙那边是教师的位子。

学生们在沙发上盘腿坐成一排。他们一起把书放在膝盖上背诵，发出一阵响亮的、调子很高的声音。

在他们能够阅读一点儿《古兰经》之后，他们开始学习写字。由于房间里没有写字台，也没有桌子，他们只能把描红本握在手里。

他们也学习语法和四则运算。

这些是他们在小学里所能得到的所有教育。大多数人对此感到满意。但是有钱人会雇佣来自欧洲其他国家的老师教导他们的孩子学习外语。

（塞缪尔·S.考克斯）

作者介绍

很多人都知道塞缪尔·S.考克斯是一位政治家，但知道他还是一位作家的人就没那么多了。他出生于俄亥俄州，但在纽约市生活了许多年。1885年，他作为美国公使出使土耳其，在那里工作了一年。他就是从那时起开始了解土耳其人的。

A Letter From India

Jeypore, January 7, 1883.

My dear Gertie:

I wish that you had been here with me yesterday. We would have had a beautiful time. You would have had to get up at five o'clock, for at six the carriage was at the door, and we had already had our breakfast. But in this country you do everything that you can very early, so as to escape the hot sun. It is very hot in the middle of the day, but quite cold now at night and in the mornings and evenings. Well, as we drove into the town, the sun rose, and the streets were full of light.

The town is all painted pink, which makes it the queerest-looking place you ever saw. On the outsides of the houses there are pictures drawn, some very solemn and some very funny.

We drove through the street, which was crowded with camels and elephants and donkeys, and women wrapped up like bundles, and men chattering like monkeys, and monkeys themselves, and little children rolling in the dust, and playing queer Jeypore games.

All the little girls, when they get to be about your age, hang jewels in their noses, and the women all have their noses looking beautiful in this way. I have a nose jewel for you, which I shall put in when I get home, and also a little button for the side of Susie's nose, such as the smaller children wear. Think how the girls at school will admire you.

Well, we drove out the other side of the queer pink town, and went on toward the old town, which they deserted a hundred years ago, when they built this.

The priest told the king that they ought not to live more than a thousand years in one place, and so, as the town was about a thousand years old, the king left it. And there it stands about five miles off, with only a few beggars and a lot of monkeys living in its splendid palaces and temples.

Behind us, as we went up the hill, came a man leading a little black goat, and when I asked what it was for, they said it was for sacrifice. It seems that a horrid old goddess has a temple on the hill, and years ago they used to sacrifice men to her, to make her happy and kind.

When we got into the old town, it was a perfect wilderness of beautiful things——lakes, temples, palaces, porticoes, all sorts of things in marble and fine stones, with sacred long-tailed monkeys running over all. I will tell you all about the goddess, and the rest that I saw, when I get home. Don't you wish that you had gone with me? Give my love to your father and mother and Agnes and Susie. I am dying to know about your Christmas and the presents. Do not forget your loving uncle.

Phillips
(Bishop Phillips Brooks)

译文

印度来的一封信

亲爱的格蒂：

真希望昨天你能和我一起在这里。那样我们就会度过一段美好的时光。你会在5点钟起床，因为马车6点钟就会到门口等候了，那时我们必须吃完早餐。在这个国度，你做任何事都要尽早，以防被炎热的太阳晒到。这里正午很热，但早晨晚上都很冷。嗯，当我们乘着马车进入小镇时，太阳升起来了，黎明的光辉铺满了街道。

整个小镇都被阳光染成了粉红色，看起来非常神奇。许多房子外面画着图画，有的画风格外庄重，有的则十分滑稽。

我们驾车穿过拥挤的街道。街上有骆驼、大象、驴子，有裹得严严实实的女人，有像猴子一般交谈的男人和真正的猴子，还有在尘土中打闹嬉戏的小孩。孩子们玩的都是稀奇古怪的杰伊布尔当地游戏。

这里的小姑娘们长到你这么大的时候，都会在鼻子那儿挂些珠宝，所有女人都会通过这种方式来展现自己的魅力。我买了个鼻饰给你，等我回家就给你戴上。我还带了个小珠钮，想给祖西戴在鼻侧，这种饰品就是给更小点的姑娘戴的。想想学校的女生们得多羡慕你吧！

嗯，我们驾着马车从古怪的粉红小镇的另一侧穿出，然后朝着老城区继续前行。一百年前老城区被遗弃时，他们建造了这座粉红小镇。

当时，牧师对国王说，他们在同一个地方居住的时间不能超过一千年。鉴于老城区就要满一千岁了，国王只好离开。于是，这座老城就永远伫立在八千米之外。只有几个乞丐和一些猴子，住在那些辉煌的宫殿和神庙里。

我们爬到山丘上的时候，身后走过来一个男人，他牵着一只黑色的小山羊。我问他这只山羊有什么用，他回答说，这是用来祭祀的。山坡上似乎有一座寺庙，供奉着古老的恐怖女神。几年前他们还曾把活人作为祭品献给她，以此取悦她。

等我们到达老城区的时候，就会看到一片美丽的景象：湖泊、寺庙、宫殿、门廊，各种各样的用大理石和其他精美的石头建造的房子，还有神圣的长尾猴从上面跑过。等我到家，我会告诉你有关这位女神的一切，还会告诉你我在这里的其他见闻。你现在是不是有点巴不得当初和我一起来了呢？代我向你的父母、阿格内斯还有苏西问好。我非常想知道你圣诞节是怎么过的，收到了哪些礼物。可别忘了你亲爱的叔叔哦。

菲利普斯

1883年1月7日，写于杰伊布尔

（毕晓普·菲利普斯·布鲁克斯）

✍ 作者介绍

毕晓普·菲利普斯·布鲁克斯，在费城和波士顿两地的教堂当了很多年的牧师。他曾在欧洲和亚洲旅游，《旅行的信》里最有趣的一些书信就是写给孩子们的。

Chinese Children and Their Games

Before I went to China, I could not but wonder, when I saw a Chinese or Japanese doll. why they made so strange-looking things for babies to play with.

When I reached the East, the whole matter was made clear to me by my first sight of a baby. The doll looks like the child!

When the child begins to walk and talk, it becomes very interesting.

Its father has a little push cart made by which it learns to walk.

The nurse goes about the court with the baby repeating "Ba Ba, Ma Ma," is correct, and it should be introduced as "which means 'Father' and 'Mother.'" She also teaches the child the names of the other members of the family.

When the boy is old enough, he grows a queue. We do not think any less of the Chinese boy for wearing his hair in this fashion.

We must remember that George Washington and Lafayette and other men of their times wore their hair in a braid down their backs.

This queue has a great many uses. The workman spreads a handkerchief or towel over his head, wraps his queue around it, and makes for himself a hat. The cart driver whips his mule with it. The beggar uses it to scare away the dogs.

The father takes hold of his little boy's queue instead of his hand, when walking with him on the street; or the child follows holding to his father's queue.

The boys use one another's queues as reins when they play horse, and they also serve in some of the other games that the boys play.

The Chinese boys and girls are little men and women. At an early age they learn the rules of conduct, which they use through life.

Their clothes are cut on the same pattern, out of the same kind of cloth as those of their parents and grandparents. There are no kilts and knee-breeches, aprons and short skirts, to make them feel that they are little people.

The nursery is well provided with rhymes about parts of the body. They have rhymes to repeat when they play with the five fingers, and others when they pull the toes; rhymes when they take hold of the knee, and expect the child to keep from laughing; rhymes about the face, and so on.

Here is a little rhyme that is as pleasing to the Chinese child as the "little pig" has always been to our children:

This little cow eats grass,
This little cow eats hay,
This little cow drinks water,
This little cow runs away,
This little cow does nothing,
Except lie down all day.
We'll whip her.

With that, the nurse or mother playfully slaps the little bare foot.

In addition to his games and rhymes, the fairs that are held in the great temples are to the Chinese boy what a fair, or a circus, or a Fourth of July is to an American farmer's boy or girl. He has his cash, or Chinese coins, for candy or fruit, and for his crackers that he fires off at New Year's time.

Kite-flying is a pleasure that no American boy cares for as much as the Chinese boy does. This pleasure clings to him until he is old, for it is not uncommon to find a child and his grandfather flying their kites together.

The Chinese child is also fond of pets. He has birds, which he carries around in cages or on a perch. He has his crickets, with which he amuses himself; and his gold fish, which bring him days and years of delight.

(Isaac Taylor Headland)

✍ 译文

中国孩子和他们的游戏

在我去中国之前，每当看见中国玩偶或是日本玩偶就忍不住好奇：为什么他们会做出这种奇形怪状的东西给小孩子玩呢？

但当我来到东方，在我看到小孩子的第一眼我就全明白了。这些小孩子和那些玩偶一模一样！

小孩子走路和说话的样子都非常有趣。

父亲准备了一辆小推车，好让孩子可以学习走路。

保姆带着小孩子在院子里走来走去，反复教孩子喊"爸爸""妈妈"。她还会教孩子称呼其他家庭成员。

男孩子到了一定岁数就会留起一条辫子。我们不要小看那些梳着辫子的男孩。

我们一定还记得在乔治·华盛顿和拉斐特那个时代，所有人都戴着垂到背部的假发。

这条辫子有很多作用。工人在头上盖上一块手帕或是一条毛巾，然后用辫子缠绕起来，就跟戴了顶帽子似的。驾车的车夫可以用辫子抽打拉车的骡子，乞丐也可以用辫子吓走野狗。

父亲和孩子一起走在街上的时候，不会拉着孩子的手，而是拉着孩子的辫子。或者，孩子跟在父亲后面，拉着父亲的辫子。

男孩们玩骑马游戏的时候，也会把对方的辫子当作马鞭。在男孩子玩的其他游戏里，辫子也是一种道具。

中国的男孩和女孩都是小大人。他们小时候学习的行为准则将会贯穿他们的一生。

他们的衣服布料是相同的，裁剪出来的款式也是相同的，就和他们的父母、祖父母当年一样。他们没有百褶裙、及膝短裤、围裙和短裙这类能让他们穿得像个小孩的衣服。

他们会教小孩子许多和身体部位有关的童谣。这些童谣有的是掰着五个手指头的时候唱的，有的是拉扯脚趾头的时候唱的，有的是抓住小孩子的膝盖、希望他们不要笑的时候唱的，还有的童谣唱的是小孩子的脸蛋，如此等等。

这里有一首童谣。中国的孩子像我们的孩子喜爱《小猪》一样喜爱它：

这个小牛吃草，

这个小牛吃料，

这个小牛喝水，

这个小牛打滚，

这个小牛竟卧着，

我们打他。

保姆或母亲会一边唱着这首歌，一边游戏似的拍打着小孩子们光着的小脚。

除了游戏和童谣，那些在大庙里举行的庙会也不能不提。对于中国的男孩子们来说，庙会是集市，是马戏，中国孩子像美国孩子喜欢独立日那样喜欢庙会（7月4日是美国独立日，也是美国的法定节日）。这一天，他会带上银两或者铜钱，去买一些糖果或是水果。他还会买点爆竹，留到新年时放。

中国的男孩们觉得放风筝充满了乐趣，没有哪个美国男孩子会这么想。鉴于许多祖父也会和孩子一起放风筝，这种快乐显然会伴随他们一生。

中国孩子也喜爱宠物。他们养鸟，会把鸟装在笼子里，或是让鸟站在栖枝上带出去遛。他们养蟋蟀，这项活动让他们颇为自得其乐；他们还养金鱼，总能从中得到乐趣。

（艾萨克·泰勒·黑德兰）

◈ 作者介绍

1890年，传教士艾萨克·泰勒·黑德兰到了中国。从那时起，他一直在北京大学担任教授。同时，他也是北京一所教堂的牧师。

黑德兰先生在中国居住了很长时间。在这段时间里，他深入了解了中国的孩子们，并在《中国的男孩女孩》《孺子歌图》和《中国的英雄》三本书中写了许多关于他们的欢快的故事。本文选自《中国的男孩女孩》一书。这些书均由弗莱·H. 利华公司出版。

The Education of a Young Prince

Near the City of Potsdam, in Germany, there is a large palace that is called Frederick the Great's "New Palace".

In the topmost story of this palace were the quarters used by the teachers of Prince William and his brother, the sailor Prince Henry, when they were boys.

To anyone that had lived in an American or an English house, the bareness of the upper story of this famous palace seemed strange.

This room was wide in space, and furnished a foretaste of the barrack life that should seem comforting to a German prince. In wet weather it made a Capital playground, and many a pane of glass was smashed by the blundering aim of one of the youngsters.

In the park, near the palace, were planted the masts and rigging of a ship. There Prince Henry was taught sailing, and the spot become a favorite romping place.

Some of us then played pirates, and made chase after a crew that had taken refuge aloft.

What was better still, we sometimes took a trip about the neighboring lakes on a small frigate. This craft looked terrible at a distance, with its scowling ports and man o'war yards, but it was really only a little larger than a good-sized ship's cutter.

The trip on this frigate was looked upon by us all as the greatest of our treats. Even today the Emperor delights in yachting, and sails his toy frigate whenever he has the chance.

When the day's romp was over, we had tea before going home, always out of doors in fair weather.

The princes' father and mother, who were afterward the Emperor and Empress Frederick, never failed to appear at these times. They said a few words to each of us, and asked after our families, or about the sports of the day.

The Empress in particular, who was then Crown Princess, always looked at our food to see that it was wholesome. She also saw that her little sons and daughters, as well as their guests, had their napkins properly tucked under their chins.

The food was of the plainest and most wholesome kind: bread or toast, fresh milk, and some simple bread, cake, perhaps with big raisins in it.

When the Crown Princess and her husband appeared, no face lit up with more pleasure than that of Prince William. I remember once-it was at tea on the steam yacht-Prince William whispered to me a fact, which he took great pride, that the cake had been made by his mother.

Of course, at these romps, the idea of expecting fine manners to be observed would have been absurd. Now and then, however, there came into these playground meetings some youngster who had been carefully drilled at home to show particular respect in the presence of the blood royal.

Such a child lived in dread of breaking some fancied rule, and moved about in a very uncomfortable way. Prince William, noted as he justly is for gentleness, could hardly hide his dislike for the little flunkies that were now and then forced upon him.

Not that he laughed at their shyness; in fact, it was he that set the new arrivals at their ease. He tried to discover their leading tastes, and played the games that would please the larger number.

When sport was once under way, it would have taken a keen observer indeed, to say that either Prince William or Prince Henry depended upon anything beyond his own head and hands to make the day successful.

It was my fortune, as an American, to be supposed to have a close acquaintance with the red savages of the Wild West. This belief I could in no way shake off, in spite of the fact that at that time I had not even seen an Indian. So it happened that I was often called upon to make plans for Indian warfare.

Prince William knew Cooper from beginning to end, and, for that matter, I was not far behind him. Our Indian studies, therefore, usually turned into playing the part of some Leather stocking heroes. In these plays we armed ourselves as queerly as possible, and then crawled through the under bush for the purpose of capturing some other party. The second party was either a tribe of enemies or a company of pale-faces.

But I have said enough to describe Prince William as a plucky, hearty, modest lad, affectionate toward his parents, and thoughtful for the youngsters of his own age with whom he was brought in touch.

(Poultney Bigelow, adapted)

译文

年轻王子的教育

离德国城市波茨坦很近的地方有一座宫殿，这个宫殿就是腓特烈二世的"新宫"。

在宫殿的最顶层住着威廉王子和"航海者"亨利王子年少时的老师。

任何一个曾住过美式房子或英式房子的人都会觉得惊讶，这样一座著名的宫殿的顶楼居然如此简朴。

顶层的屋子很宽敞，是按照军营的风格来装修的，看来德国王子住在这儿会感到很舒适。在下雨的天气，这儿就是主要的聚会活动场所。因为某个小孩子乱砸窗户，许多窗户的玻璃都碎了。

在宫殿不远处的花园里，放置着一艘船的桅杆和绳索。亨利王子就是在这学会航船的。这儿也是孩子们最喜爱的玩耍场地。

一些人装成海盗，另一些人假扮船员。船员假装将难民救走，海盗在后面追逐着船员。

还有些时候更有意思，我们会坐上小型护卫舰，到周围的湖里游玩。远远看去，这艘船显得十分可怕，因为它的港口和主力舰都阴沉沉的，但其实它也就比一艘一般的大舰艇大上这么一丁点儿。

我们觉得，国王对我们热情招待，才会让我们坐着舰船航行。即使到了今天，国王也很喜欢航行，一有机会就坐上他的迷你舰艇。

一天的游玩结束时，如果天气很好，我们往往一起到户外去，在回家之前再喝一杯茶。

一般在这种时候，王子的父亲和母亲，也就是后来的腓特烈国王和腓特烈王后，都会和我们一起喝茶。他们会跟我们随便聊几句，问问我们的家里情况，或者谈谈当天的各项游玩活动情况。

  王后当时还是女王储，她总会检查我们的食物，确保食物是卫生的。她还会盯着她的儿女们以及客人们，确保他们都把餐巾按照正确的方式叠在他们的下巴下面。

  一般来说，大家吃的都是一些最普通、最安全的东西，如吐司面包、新鲜牛奶、普通的面包、蛋糕，有时候里面还有葡萄干呢。

  女王储和她的丈夫在场的时候，威廉王子是最开心的。我记得有次我们在舰艇上喝茶时，威廉王子对我耳语，他骄傲地告诉我，我们吃的蛋糕是他母亲亲手做的。

  当然，在这些活动过程中，我们是无法期待所有人都彬彬有礼。但是，在聚会中，总会有一些很有家教的年轻人在皇室面前表现得恭敬有礼。

  有一些孩子畏畏缩缩，生怕做错了什么，因而显得非常不自然。威廉王子素以仪态万方著称，他对那些不时冲撞自己的孩子有一种几乎无法掩饰的讨厌。

  威廉王子并不会嘲笑这些羞涩的孩子，事实上，他还会想方设法，让新客人不感到拘束。威廉王子会努力找出大家共同的喜好，然后带领大家一起玩适合绝大多数人参与的游戏。

  有观察力的人会发现，当大家一起游戏的时候，威廉王子和亨利王子会尽自己的力量让这一天过得愉快。

  作为一个美国人，能够熟悉"西大荒"的野人，我感到非常幸运。尽管在那之前我从来没有见过印第安人，我却始终坚信这一点。当人们邀请我为印第安人战争制定作战计划的时候，我也没有同意。

  威廉王子对詹姆斯·库柏的作品非常了解，因此，我也对库柏非常熟悉。于是，我们常常在一起扮演《皮袜子故事集》中的主人公。在那些剧本角色中，我们尽可能穿上奇形怪状的衣服，在丛林中爬行，去追捕另一方的人。一般追捕的对象都是其他部落的敌人或者一群"白鬼子"（译注：印第安人眼中的白种人）。

  关于威廉王子，我已经介绍得够多了，他是一个对父母热心、谦逊、饱含深情的好儿子，同时也是一位非常体贴的同龄朋友。

（波尔特尼·比奇洛，有删改）

Chapter 2

Legends&Story and Adventure | 传奇和历险故事

预习

Britain /ˈbrɪtn/ 不列颠人
handle /ˈhændl/ 柄
means /miːnz/ 意味着
precious /ˈpreʃəs/ 珍贵的
satin /ˈsætn/ 绸缎
scabbard /ˈskæbərd/ 剑鞘
sorely /ˈsɔːrli/ 严重地
wounded /ˈwuːndɪd/ 受伤

King Arthur and the Sword Excalibur

Now it happened after Arthur had become King of Britain, that he met a strange knight upon the road, and broke his sword in battle with him.

As he rode away wounded from the battle, Arthur said to his friend Merlin, "Now I have no sword. What shall I do?"

"Do not fear," said Merlin. "Nearby is a sword that shall be yours."

So they rode till they came to a lake, which was a fair lake——very beautiful and broad. In the middle of the lake, King Arthur saw an arm clothed in white satin, holding above the water a bright sword.

"Lo, yonder is the sword of which I spoke," said Merlin.

Just then they saw a lady in the lake.

"Who is that?" said Arthur.

"That is the Lady of the Lake," said Merlin. "She will come to you, and then you can ask her to give you that sword."

Soon she came, and King Arthur bowed to her. "Lady," said he, "what sword is that, which the white arm holds shining above the water? I wish it were mine, for I have no sword."

"Sir king," said the lady, "that sword is mine, and if you will give me a gift when I ask it of you, you shall have it."

The king agreed to this. Then the lady told him to step into a boat that was near, and row out and get the sword and its scabbard.

King Arthur and Merlin at once tied their horses, got into the boat, and rowed toward the sword. When they came to it, the king took it by the handle, and carried it away with him. The arm and hand went under the water.

Merlin told the king that the name of the sword was Excalibur, which means cut-steel. He also told him that the scabbard was more precious than the sword, for while he wore the scabbard he could lose no blood, no matter how sorely wounded he was.

(Thomas Malory)

译文

亚瑟王和神剑

亚瑟成为不列颠的国王之后,在路上遇见了一个陌生的骑士,亚瑟王和他决斗,弄断了自己的圣剑。

在决斗中不幸负伤的亚瑟王只能骑马逃走。他问自己的朋友梅林:"怎么办?我现在没有剑了。"

"别担心,"梅林安慰道,"这附近有一把剑,很快就会归你所有。"

于是,他们继续赶路,直到看见一片湖,才停下来。这片湖宽阔美丽,湖水清澈见底。亚瑟王发现,在湖的正中央,有一截穿着白色绸衣的手臂露出了水面,手中握着一把闪闪发光的宝剑。

"瞧,我刚刚说的那把剑就在那边。"梅林对亚瑟王说。

就在这时,他们看到湖面上出现了一位仙女。

"她是谁?"亚瑟问梅林。

"她是湖中仙子，"梅林回答道，"一会儿她就会走过来，到时候你就可以请她把剑给你。"

很快，湖中仙子就过来了。亚瑟王向她鞠了个躬，说道："仙女，请问，湖中央的手里的那把剑是什么剑？我的剑没了，我很想要这把剑。"

"尊敬的国王，"仙女说，"那把剑是我的，不过，如果你能送我一样我想要的东西，我就会把剑给你。至于是什么东西，我在需要的时候会跟你说的。"

亚瑟王答应了仙女的条件。于是，仙女告诉他们，可以搭乘旁边的小船，把船划到湖中央去拿那把剑和剑鞘。

亚瑟王和梅林赶忙把马拴在了一旁，坐上船，向湖中央划去。到了那里，亚瑟王抓住剑柄，轻轻一拿，剑就到了他手里。刚刚抓着剑的那只手慢慢沉到了水中。

梅林告诉亚瑟王，这把剑被称为断钢之剑，意为剑之锋刃，可削铁如泥。他还说，这把剑的剑鞘比剑本身更为珍贵，如果谁能佩戴断钢之剑的剑鞘，即使身负重伤，也能滴血不流。

（托马斯·马洛里）

✍ 作者介绍

托马斯·马洛里是威尔士人。他从儿时起，就知道关于亚瑟王的种种传说。

他的代表作《亚瑟王与圆桌骑士》是最早的英语出版物之一。其中《亚瑟王与神剑》（见于第二册），《断钢之剑》和《加哈拉德爵士》这几个故事，能在《孩子们的亚瑟王》或其他类似书籍中读到。

✍ 练习

把下列陈述句改为问句。

(1) The name of the sword is Excalibur.

_____

(2) The king was wounded in battle.

_____

Sir Galahad and the Round Table

There has never been such a brave band of knights as those who gathered about the Round Table of King Arthur long years ago in a country far away.

One could not be a knight unless he was strong and brave and true. Knights spent their time seeking to do some brave, good thing. If some dragon stood in the path, they swept him away. If someone was in danger or suffering wrong, they rushed to the rescue.

They found out the poor and needy and helped the sick, and thought of others first and themselves last. Through the green woods and the meadows, in plumed hats and bright armor, they rode on beautiful horses.

Little children listened for their bugle blasts, and shouted the names of those they loved : "Sir Launcelot! Sir Galahad! Sir Percival!"

The Round Table, about which they sometimes gathered in the evening, with Arthur at the head, had come to the King as a wedding gift. One hundred and fifty knights could be seated around it.

One by one the seats were filled until there were left only three-reserved for the three greatest knights of all. Sir Launcelot and Sir Percival were placed in two of these seats, but for a long time one still remained empty.

The empty seat was feared by the knights, for if anyone but the right person sat in this seat, he lost his life.

Then one day, an old man came, bringing with him a young knight. "Sir," said this man to King Arthur, "I bring you here a young knight of noble blood. He shall aid you in doing great things."

"You are welcome," said the King, "and the young knight with you."

The old man then led the young knight to the empty seat, called the Perilous Seat. The silken cloth that had been thrown over the chair was lifted up, and these words were found: "This is the seat of Sir Galahad, the good knight." Now Sir Galahad was the name of this very knight.

"Sir," said the old man, "this place is yours," and he put the young knight into the seat. Then, turning to the knights, the old man said, "Sir Galahad is the knight by whom the Holy Grail shall be found."

The young knight sat in the seat without fear. Then the knights wondered, for no man had ever dared to sit in that seat but one, and a flame had leaped forth and devoured him.

Then came King Arthur to Sir Galahad and said, "Sir, you are welcome to the Round Table, for you shall move many good knights unto the quest of the Holy Grail. You shall achieve also, what no other knight has been able to do."

(Thomas Malory)

译文

加哈拉德与圆桌骑士

在很久很久以前，有一个遥远的国家。在这个国家，国王亚瑟的圆桌周围总是聚集着一群骑士。世上再没有谁比他们更勇敢无畏了。

每一名骑士都必须坚强、英勇、忠诚。他们行为英勇，伸张正义。假如一条龙挡住了人们的去路，他们立即上前把它赶走；假如有人身处险境，或者无故受难，他们会挺身而出，奋力搭救。

他们总是先人后己，帮助那些亟须援手的贫病之人。他们头戴有羽饰的帽子，身穿闪闪发光的盔甲，骑着高头大马穿行在绿色的树林中和广袤的草原上。

孩子们一听到骑士们吹响号角，就会欢呼着高喊他们敬仰的人的名字："兰斯洛特！加哈拉德！帕西瓦尔！"

有时候他们在晚上举行圆桌会议，亚瑟王坐在主位，骑士们则坐在圆桌周围。这张大圆桌是亚瑟王结婚时收到的贺礼，可以坐上一百五十名骑士。

骑士们一个接一个地坐进了椅子，只剩下三名最伟大的骑士的位子还空着。后来，兰斯洛特和帕西瓦尔陆续坐到他们的椅子里，但剩下一个座位却迟迟没有人坐。

骑士们都不敢坐这个空座位，因为假如自己配不上这个位置，就会危及生命。

一天，一位老人带着一名年轻的骑士走了进来。"国王陛下！"他向亚瑟王致意道，"我为您带来了一位出身高贵的年轻骑士，他愿意帮助您完成伟业。"

亚瑟王回答说："欢迎你，还有这位年轻的骑士。"

老人领着年轻骑士走向那被称为"危坐"的空位子，他揭开覆盖在椅子上的绸布，椅子上顿时显现出一行字："这是伟大骑士加哈拉德的座位"。从现在起，这名年轻骑士的名字就叫加哈拉德了。

"这就是您的位子。"老人边说边把年轻骑士按到了座位上，然后他转向骑士们说，"只有加哈拉德，才能找到圣杯"。

年轻骑士毫不畏惧地坐在椅子里，骑士们大感惊奇，因为迄今为止还没有谁敢坐在那个位子上。曾经有人觊觎这个位子，但一束火焰立即从座位上升了起来，将他吞没了。

亚瑟王走向加哈拉德说："很高兴你成为圆桌骑士的一员。你要带领这些英勇的骑士去追寻圣杯，直到找到为止。除了你，没有哪个骑士能完成这一壮举。"

（托马斯·马洛里）

The Holy Grail

And one there was among us, ever moved,
Among us in white armor, Galahad.
"God make thee beautiful as thou are beautiful,"
Said Arthur, when he dubbed him knight, and none,
In so young youth, was ever made a knight.
Till Galahad.

(Alfred Tennyson)

译文

圣杯

我们中间曾有一个令人感动的骑士，
那就是穿着白色盔甲的加哈拉德。
亚瑟王授予他真正的骑士称号，
告诉他："上帝赋予了你应得的美好。"
他是骑士中，最年轻的一个。
他就是加哈拉德。

（阿尔弗雷德·丁尼生）

Daniel

It pleased Darius to set over the kingdom an hundred and twenty princes, which should be over the whole kingdom; and over these three presidents; of whom, Daniel was first; that the princes might give accounts unto them and the king should have no damage.

Then this Daniel was preferred above the presidents and princes, because an excellent spirit was in him; and the king thought to set him over the whole realm.

Then the presidents and princes sought to find occasion against Daniel concerning the kingdom; but they could find none occasion nor fault; for as much as he was faithful, neither was there any error or fault found in him.

Then said these men, We shall not find any occasion against this Daniel, except we find it against him concerning the law of his God.

Then these presidents and princes assembled together to the king, and said thus unto him, King Darius, live forever.

All the presidents of the kingdom, the governors, and the princes, the counselors, and the captains, have consulted together to establish a royal statute, and to make a firm decree, that whosoever shall ask a petition of any God or man for thirty days, save of thee, O king, he shall be cast into the den of lions.

Now, O king, establish the decree, and sign the writing, that it be not changed, according to the law of the Medes and Persians, which altered not. Wherefore King Darius signed the writing and the decree.

Now when Daniel knew that the writing was signed, he went into his house; and his windows being open in his chamber toward Jerusalem, he kneeled upon his knees three times a day, and prayed, and gave thanks before his God as he did aforetime.

Then these men assembled, and found Daniel praying and making supplication before his God.

Then they came near, and spake before the king concerning the king's decree. Hast thou not signed a decree, that every man that shall ask a petition of any God or man within thirty days, save of thee, O king, shall be cast into the den of lions?

The king answered and said, The thing is true, according to the law of the Medea and Persians which altereth not.

Then answered they and said, before the king, That Daniel, which is of the children of the captivity of Judah, regardeth not thee, O king, nor the decree that thou hast signed, but maketh his petition three times a day.

Then the king, when he heard these words, was sore displeased with himself, and set his heart on Daniel to deliver him.

Then these men assembled unto the king, and said unto the king: Know, O king, that the law of the Modes and Persians is, That no decree nor statute which the king establisheth may be changed.

Then the king commanded, and they brought Daniel, and cast him into the den of lions. Now the king spake and said unto Daniel, Thy God whom thou servest continually, he will deliver thee.

And a stone was brought, and laid upon the mouth of the den; and the king sealed it with his own signet, and with the signet of his lords; that the purpose might not be changed concerning Daniel.

Then the king went to his palace, and passed the night fasting: neither were instruments of music brought before him: and his sleep went from him. Then the king arose very early in the morning, and went in haste unto the den of lions.

And when he came to the den, he cried with a lamentable voice unto Daniel: and the king spake and said to Daniel, O Daniel, servant of the living God, is thy God, whom thou servest continually, able to deliver thee from the lions? Then said Daniel unto the king, O king, live forever. My God hath sent his angel, and bath shut the lions' mouths, that they have not hurt me; for as much as before him innocency was found in me; and also before thee, O king, have I done no hurt.

Then was the king exceeding glad for him, and commanded that they should take Daniel up out of the den. So Daniel was taken up out of the den, and no manner of hurt was found upon him, because he believed in his God.

译文

但以理

依大流士所愿，全国上下共设立一百二十个总督，来统管国中事务；在他们之上又设立三个总长（但以理位居首席），处理总督事务，使王免遭损害。

但以理因心生聪慧灵性，在总督、总长中受偏宠。王甚至考虑授之整个王土。

那时总督与总长们伺机想以国事弹劾但以理，但是他为人忠厚至极，竟无半点过失和疏忽，更不用提什么错误与罪过了。

于是这些人说，除非我们能找到他做下的与他信奉的神律相违之事，否则不可能找到任何弹劾他的理由。

这些总督与总长便在王前聚集起来，进言说："吾王大流士万岁。"

国中所有总长、钦差、总督、谋士和巡抚彼此商议，共同建立至高无上的法规，并坚决推行禁令，三十日之内，不论何人，但凡敢向任何神或其他什么人祈福祷告，啊，王在上，必将其投入狮子穴之中。

啊，我的王，此刻，就请你立下法规，签署无法变更的禁令，依玛代与波斯人的例，法令不可更改。于是，大流士王批准了这项法规。

但以理得知这项禁令，回到家中；而房中的窗户正对耶路撒冷敞开着。他双膝跪地，一日三次，向上帝跪拜、祈祷、感恩，和以前并无两样。

于是那些人聚集而来，发现但以理正在上帝面前祈愿恳求。

他们觐见，对王提起那条禁令，说："您不是已经下令了吗？三十日之内，任何向其他什么神或人祈愿的人，不论是谁，都要将其投入狮子穴中的。"

王说："依玛代与波斯人的法令，确有此事。"

于是他们又说："王啊，在您面前，那但以理，那囚禁之徒犹太人的后代，无视您，我的王，无视您签署的禁令，竟每日祷告三次。"

王听到这番话，虽痛心不已，但一心只想解救但以理。

那时，那些人就联合起来，劝王说："啊，我的王，您当知，玛代与波斯人有例，那法规和禁令，一旦签订，永不更改。"

于是王只好下令，将但以理带走，投入狮子穴之中。王对但以理说："你平素侍奉的那上帝，他会解救你。"

人们搬来石块，放在狮子穴的出口；王用他那象征王权的印章，以及大臣的印章封印了出口；但以理的命运已经注定。

王回到他的宫殿，草草度过这一晚，也无心欣赏音乐；整夜难以安寝。次日黎明，王早早起来，匆忙赶往狮子穴。

他来到狮子穴，悲戚地呼喊但以理："啊，但以理，永生神的仆从，那位上帝，你平素侍奉的神，他可将你从狮子口中解救？"但以理对王说："啊，我的王，愿你永生。我的上帝派遣他的天使，将狮口封住，使它们无法伤害我；只因我在他面前是无罪的；我的王啊，在您的面前，我也是无害的。"

于是王甚是欢喜，还命令他们将但以理从狮子穴中救出。但以理因此从洞穴中获救，毫发无损，只因他信奉上帝。

Trout Fishing

There was one little river, and only one, within the Boy's knowledge, and the reach of his short legs. It was a tiny rivulet that came out of the woods about half a mile away from the hotel, and ran down through a sloping meadow, crossing the road under a flat bridge of boards.

Those rapids and those pools, with beautiful foam on them like soft, white custard,——were they not such places as the trout loved to hide in? So the Boy slips past the house, with a bamboo pole over his shoulder, and a little brother in skirts and short white stockings, tagging along behind him.

What an afternoon! How tired the adventurers grow as the day wears away! Yet they have taken nothing! But their strength and courage return when there comes a surprising twitch at the line. With a jerk of the pole, a small, wiggling fish is whirled through the air and landed back in the meadow.

"For pity's sake, don't lose him! There he is among the roots of the blue flag."

"I've got him! How cold he is! How slippery! How pretty! Just like a piece of rainbow!"

"Do you see the red spots? Did you notice how gamy he was, Little Brother; how he played? It is a trout for sure; a real trout, and almost as long as your hand."

So the two lads, chattering, tramp along up the stream. Presently another trout falls a victim, and then they begin to wish for something larger.

In the very last pool that they dare attempt, the Boy drags out the hoped-for prize. It is a splendid trout, longer than a new lead pencil. But he feels sure that there must be another, even larger, in the same place.

He swings his line out carefully over the water. Just as he is about to drop it in, Little Brother, perched on the sloping brink, slips on the smooth pine-needles, and goes sliding down into the pool up to his waist.

How he weeps with dismay, and how funnily his dress sticks to him as he crawls out! But his grief is soon lessened by the privilege of carrying the trout strung on an alder twig. So it is a happy, muddy, pair of urchins that climb over the fence out of the field of triumph at the close of the day.

(Henry van Dyke)

译文

钓鱼历险记

男孩知道，他凭双脚就能走到的小河只有一条。那里离旅馆大约八百米，一条窄细的溪水从树林里流出，沿着倾斜的草地蜿蜒而下，穿过了平板桥下方的道路。

湍急的水流撞击出一个个水洼，美丽的泡沫就像软绵绵的雪白奶油。——这不是鳟鱼最喜欢躲藏的地方吗？于是男孩溜出家门去，肩上扛着一根竹竿，他的小弟弟在他身后紧跟着，穿着连衣裙和白色的短袜。

这个下午可真倒霉啊！时间一点点过去，他们倍感疲惫，却什么都没钓着！但是，钓线出人意料地颤动了一下，这时，他们的力气和勇气瞬间就回来了。男孩猛地拉了一下钓竿，一条颤抖的小鱼从空中翻腾而过，向后落在草地上。

"看在老天的份上，可别让他跑了！他就掉在蓝菖蒲的底下。"

"我抓到他了！他身上真冷，还滑溜溜的，简直太可爱了！他就像一片彩虹！"

"弟弟，你看见那个红点了吗？你看他多么勇敢，使劲扭动着身体想要逃跑。这肯定是条鳟鱼，一条真正的鳟鱼，几乎跟你的手掌一样大。"

两个小家伙沿着小溪边走边聊，很快他们就钓到了另外一只小鳟鱼。之后，他们不禁期望着能钓上一条更大的。

在最后一个他们敢于涉足的水洼中，男孩终于拉出一条他盼望许久的大鳟鱼。它可真大，身体比一支新铅笔还长。但他感觉在这里应该还有一条比这更大的鳟鱼。

他小心翼翼地将钓线抛向水面，就在钓线入水的时候，原本坐在斜坡边缘的小弟弟在滑溜溜的松叶上滑了一下，跌倒在齐腰深的水洼里。

他恼羞成怒地哭了起来。而且，他爬出来的时候，裙子紧紧贴在身上，样子太好笑了！不过，他在水里抓到一条杨树枝上挂着的鳟鱼之后，很快就高兴了起来。天快黑的时候，这两个小淘气鬼终于带着一身泥泞爬过篱笆，胜利归来，快乐无比。

（亨利·范·戴克）

练习

1.以感叹号结尾、表达惊讶、好奇、愉快或者痛苦的句子，是感叹句。用 oh, alas, how, what, nonsense 各造一个感叹句。

2.给印度的孩子写一封信，描写你的家乡。

Thinking Only of Myself

Once there was a man who thought his whole duty was in serving himself. This he did, and became very poor.

In fact, the more he toiled, the poorer he became. At last he found himself, his wife, and his children without a single cent.

So he went to a wise man to seek his fate. This wise man lived in a forest temple far, far away, and the journey to this temple was rough and dangerous.

In the jungle the poor man met a camel with two sacks of treasure on his back.

"Where are you going?" asked the camel.

"To seek my fate," said the man.

"Ask mine, too," said the camel, "I was lost from the caravan, and I have carried these sacks of gold on my back for twelve years. I cannot lie down. Ask mine, too."

"I will," said the man. And he went on.

Then he came to a wide river in which was a great alligator.

"Take me across," said the man.

"I will," said the alligator. "where are you going ? "

"To seek my fate."

"Ask mine, too. For twelve years I have had a burning pain, and I cannot rest. Ask mine, too."

"I will," said the man. And he went on his way.

As he journeyed, he found a tiger lying in a thicket in great pain. He was surrounded by the treasures of the men that he had eaten.

"Where are you going?" asked the tiger.

"To seek my fate."

"Ask mine, also, for I have had this thorn in my foot for twelve years. I cannot rest. Ask mine, also."

"I will," said the man.

At last the man reached the temple of fate.

"What do you seek here?" asked the wise old priest.

"I seek my fate. I have twelve children, and am very poor."

"Then you must have been living only for yourself. Think only of making others rich, and you will become rich yourself."

Then the man asked the fate of the camel.

"Take the sacks off his back, and both of you will be relieved. Why did you not do it before?"

"I was thinking only of myself," said the man.

Then he asked the fate of the alligator.

"Give him herbs," said the priest, "and both of you will be relieved. Why did you not do it before?"

"I was thinking only of myself." Then he asked the fate of the tiger.

"Take the thorn out of his foot, and both of you will be relieved. Why did you not think of that before?"

"I was thinking only of myself," said the man.

Then the man returned to the tiger.

"Have you found my fate?" asked the tiger.

The man drew the thorn out of the tiger's foot, and started to go on.

"Here, take the treasure," said the tiger. "I did not think of it before." So the man took the treasure, and hastened to the river where he had seen the alligator.

"Have you found my fate?" asked the alligator. "I am burning up."

The man found a few herbs, and gave them to the alligator. They made the alligator sick, and he cast up a ruby.

The man started on.

"Stop," said the alligator, "and take the ruby. It will make you rich."

The man took the ruby. He came at last to the camel.

"Have you found my fate?" asked the camel.

The man took the two sacks from the camel's back, and started on.

"Stop!" said the camel. "These sacks are full of gold. Take them, and both of us will be happy."

The man took the sacks of gold. By the time that he reached home, he was so rich that it took all his twelve children to help him to use his wealth.

This wealth was always used for the good of others, so that the man might not again become poor. And he never again did become poor.

(Hezekiah Butterworth)

译文

怎能只想着自己

从前有个男人认为，自己一生最重要的事就是为自己谋利。他事事都想到自己，结果却一贫如洗。

事实上，他越是辛苦劳作，越是潦倒不堪。直到有一天，他发现不管是他，他的妻子，还是他的孩子们，口袋里都没有一分钱。

于是他踏上旅途，去找一名智者，追问自己的命运。这名智者住在一座遥远的林间寺庙里，而通往寺庙的路上遍地凶险，充满艰难。

这个穷困的可怜人到达了一片丛林，在这里遇见了一只背上驮着两麻袋财宝的骆驼。

骆驼问他说："你到哪儿去呀？"

男人回答："去追寻我的命运。"

"也问一问我的命运吧。"骆驼说，"我迷路了，不知道怎么回到沙漠商队去。十二年了，我每天都驮着这两麻袋金币，根本没办法躺下来休息一会儿。也问一问我的命运吧。"

"好的。"男人答应了，继续向目标前进。

他来到一条宽广的大河边。一只巨大的鳄鱼在河里看着他。

"载我过河吧。"男人请求道。

鳄鱼答应了，说："我会的，但是你要去哪儿呢？"

"去追寻我的命运。"

"啊，请你也帮我询问一下吧。十二年来，我每天都忍受着炽热的疼痛，一刻都不能平静下来。"

"好的。"男人答应着，告别鳄鱼后继续他的旅途。

有一天在路上，他遇到了一只老虎。他躺在一片灌木丛中，显得痛苦不堪，周围堆满了他吃掉的人留下的财产。

老虎问他说："你到哪儿去？"

"去追寻我的命运。"

"帮我也问一问吧。我脚上有一根刺，折磨了我十二年。我一刻都不能安宁。"

"好的。"男人答应道。

经过漫长的跋涉之后，这个人终于到达了智者居住的命运神庙。

"你来这里做什么？"充满智慧的老祭司问他。

"追寻我的命运。我有十二个孩子，可我很穷很穷。"

"那你一定是只为自己活着。只有当你想着帮助别人致富的时候，你自己才会变得富有。"

男人恍然大悟，接着问起了骆驼的命运。

"只要你帮他拿掉背上的麻袋，你们就都能摆脱困境了。为什么你之前不这么做呢？"

男人惭愧地低下了头，说："我只想着我自己了。"

他又问起鳄鱼的命运。

祭司回答："只要你给他药草，你们就都能摆脱困境了。你之前怎么没想到呢？"

男人更惭愧了，低声说："我只想着我自己了。"接着他又问起了老虎的命运。

"只要你帮他把刺从脚里挑出来，你们就都能摆脱困境了。你之前怎么没想到呢？"

男人回答说："我只想着我自己了。"

于是他踏上了归途，首先来到了老虎身边。

"怎么样？"老虎问他。

男人将老虎脚上的刺挑了出来，准备继续往回走。

老虎说："嘿，拿上这些财宝吧。我之前怎么没想到呢？"于是男人带着老虎送给他的财宝赶到了河边。鳄鱼正等着他呢。

"帮我问了吗？"鳄鱼说，"我感觉痛得像火烧一样。"

男人找了一些草药喂给鳄鱼。这些草药让鳄鱼想吐，于是他吐出来一颗红宝石。

解决了鳄鱼的问题后，男人打算继续上路。

"等等！"鳄鱼说，"拿上这块宝石，它会让你变成有钱人。"

于是男人带上宝石继续赶路，最后回到了遇见骆驼的地方。

骆驼问他说："你有没有替我问智者，我的问题该怎么解决？"

男人没有回答，只是走过去将两个沉重的麻袋扛了下来，然后继续赶路。

骆驼说："等一下，这些麻袋里面装满了金子。我把它们送给你，这样我们都会很开心。"

男人扛起了装满金子的麻袋。等到他回到家的时候，他带回了许多金银财宝，富得流油。即使他的十二个孩子一起，依然花不完这些财富。

他总是用这些财富去帮助别人，再也不会因为只想着自己而变穷了。

（赫齐卡亚·巴特沃斯）

✍ 作者介绍

赫齐卡亚·巴特沃斯是美国杂志《青年人之友》的资深编辑之一，在年轻人当中很有声望。他非常喜欢长途旅行，还把自己在旅行中的见闻记录下来。他写了一套十二本的《曲折的旅途》，里面记录了许多有趣的旅行故事。巴特沃斯先生出生于罗德岛州，后来定居于波士顿。

Chapter 3
Poems of the Seasons | 咏叹四季

预习

butterfly /ˈbʌtərflaɪ/ 蝴蝶
crocus /ˈkroʊkəs/ 番红花
goldenrod /ˈɡoʊldənˌrɒd/ 黄花
pumpkin /ˈpʌmpkɪn/ 南瓜
rough /rʌf/ 恶劣的
throat /θroʊt/ 喉咙
twine /twaɪn/ 蜿蜒

Under the Greenwood Tree

Under the greenwood tree
Who loves to lie with me,
And turn his merry note
Unto the sweet bird's throat—
Come hither, come hither, come hither!
Here shall he see
No enemy
But winter and rough weather.

Who doth ambition shun
And loves to live in the sun,
Seeking the food he eats
And pleased with what he gets—
Come hither, come hither, come hither!
Here shall he see

No enemy
But winter and rough weather.

(William Shakespeare)

译文

绿树荫下

绿树高张翠幕，
谁来偕我偃卧，
翻将欢乐心，
学唱枝鸟鸣——
盍来此，盍来此，盍来此
目之所接，
精神契一，
唯忧雨雷之将至。

谁能敝履尊荣，
来沐丽日光风，
觅食自求果腹，
一饱欣然意足——
盍来此，盍来此，盍来此！
目之所接，
精神契一，
唯忧雨雷之将至。

（威廉·莎士比亚）

✍ 作者介绍

威廉·莎士比亚是英国最杰出的诗人。他生活在三百多年前,那时候伊丽莎白女王和詹姆斯一世国王统治着英国。

莎士比亚的作品有诗歌和戏剧。《绿树荫下》选自喜剧《皆大欢喜》。他的部分戏剧被查尔斯·兰姆和玛丽·兰姆改编成了故事集。

Crocuses

There fell an April shower, one night;
Next morning, in the garden bed,
The crocuses stood straight and gold;
"And they have come," the children said.

There fell an April shower, one night;
Next morning, through the woodland spread,
The May-flowers, pink and sweet as youth;
"And they have come," the children said.

(Mary E. Wilkins)

译文

番红花

四月里的夜晚，突降一场大雨；
在第二天早晨的花圃里，
番红花立在那里，光彩四溢；
孩子们都在说："它们来了！"

四月的夜晚，突降一场大雨；
在第二天早晨的森林里，
五月之花蔓延，像青春般粉红甜蜜；
孩子们都在说："它们来了！"

（玛丽·E. 威尔金斯）

Goldenrod

Spring is the morning of the year,
And summer is the noontide bright;
The autumn is the evening clear,
That comes before the winter's night.

And in the evening, everywhere,
Along the roadside, up and down,
I see the golden torches flare,
Like lighted street-lamps in the town.

I think the butterfly and bee,
From distant meadows coming back,
Are quite contented when they see,
These lamps along the homeward track.

But those who stay too late get lost;
For when the darkness falls about,
Down every lighted street the frost,
Will go and put the torches out!

(Frank Dempster Sherman)

译文

黄花

春是一年之晨,
夏是正午的明媚,
秋是傍晚的清澈,
然后冬夜便会来临。

至傍晚，每一处
沿着路边，上上下下，
我看见跳跃的金黄火焰，
宛如镇上点亮的街灯。

我想，蝴蝶和蜜蜂，
从远处的草地上飞回，
它们当欢欣愉悦，
因通往家的路上亮着灯。

但那些深夜归者，却迷了路；
因为当夜幕降临，
每条被照亮的街上，
大雾弥漫，火焰也熄灭了！

（弗兰克·登普斯特·谢尔曼）

🎵 作者介绍

弗兰克·登普斯特·谢尔曼是哥伦比亚大学建筑系教授，他创作了大量儿童诗歌。《黄花》以及其他诗歌收录于《小民谣》中。

Autumn

The hills are bright with maples yet,
But down the level land,
The beech leaves rustle in the wind,
As dry and brown as sand.

The clouds in bars of rusty red,
Along the hilltops glow,
And in the still sharp air the frost,
Is like a dream of snow.

The berries of the brier-rose,
Have lost their rounded pride;
The bitter-sweet chrysanthemums,
Are drooping, heavy-eyed.

The pigeons in black wavering lines,
Are swinging toward the sun;
And all the black and withered fields,
Proclaim the summer done.

His store of nuts and acorns now,
The squirrel hastes to gain,
And sets his house in order for,
The winter's dreary reign.

It's time to light the evening fire,
To read good books, to sing,
The low and lovely songs that breathe,
Of the eternal spring.

(Alice Cary)

译文

秋

枫叶已染红山冈，
而山下平原的榉树叶，
却在风中沙沙作响，
像沙子般枯干焦黄。

团团云彩铁锈一般红，
闪着亮光挂在山头，
冰冷刺骨的寒风中，
冰霜好比是雪做的一场梦。

野玫瑰的果实，
已经不再骄傲丰满；
又苦又甜的菊花，
神采尽失，正黯然凋零。

鸽子飞成左摇右晃的黑线，
朝着太阳挥动翅膀；
所有枯败的黑色田野，
都在宣告夏天的终结。

该贮存松子和橡果了，
松鼠急忙到处找，
还要拾掇他的房子，
因为冬天沉闷又无聊。

那时就在晚上点起火，

读一本好书，唱一首歌
低沉美妙的歌声吞吐，
不朽的春的气息。

（爱丽丝·卡里）

✍ 作者介绍

爱丽丝·卡里生活在俄亥俄州，她的妹妹菲比则住在纽约市。她们给杂志创作了许多故事和诗歌。菲比·卡里还有一首有趣的短诗，叫作《妒忌的鹡鸰》，也收录在本书中。

The Story of a Seed

I. The Seed.
Just a little seed,
Very small indeed;
Put it in the ground,
In a little mound,
And wait to see,
What it will be.

II. The Vine
The seed became a lovely vine,
That over the brown earth used to twine,
And at our feet so very low,
Went on and on, to grow and grow.

III. The Flower
The summer rain, the summer shine,
That wet and warmed the pretty vine,
Had somehow quite a wondrous power,
Which wrought this lovely yellow flower.

IV. The Fruit
The little flower grew and grew,
In sun and shower, and moistening dew,
And when the leaves began to fall,
There lay this gorgeous yellow ball,
The prize for harvest, best of all.

V. The Pie.
Hurrah for the tiny seed!
Hurrah for the flower and vine!

Hurrah for the golden pumpkin,
Yellow and plump and fine!
But better than all beginnings,
Surely no one can deny,
Is the end of the whole procession——
This glorious pumpkin pie.

译文

种子的故事

（一）种子
一颗小种子,
真是非常小。
放在土地上,
种进泥堆里,
等待之后看,
长成什么样。

（二）藤蔓
种子变成可爱的藤蔓,
在褐色的土地上蜿蜒爬过,
如此低微地匍匐在我们脚下,
却一刻不停地长啊长啊。

（三）花朵
夏日里的雨水和阳光,
赐予藤蔓湿润和温暖,
有一种非常奇妙的力量,
让这朵可爱的黄花开放。

（四）果实
小小花朵不停地长，
在太阳下，在大雨里，在露水中，
而当叶子开始飘零，
留在那儿的美丽的黄色小球，
是丰收的最好奖赏。

（五）馅饼
小小的种子好棒！
花朵和藤蔓好棒！
金色的南瓜好棒！
又黄又圆又漂亮！
还有比这一切更好的，
谁也不会不认账，
最后的时刻已经来临——
南瓜馅饼真是甜香。

March

The cock is crowing,
The stream is flowing,
The small birds twitter,
The lake doth glitter,
The green field sleeps in the sun;
The oldest and youngest
Are at work with the strongest;
The cattle are grazing,
Their heads never raising;
There are forty feeding like one.

Like an army defeated,
The snow hath retreated,
And now doth fare ill,
On the top of the bare hill;
The plowboy is whooping—anon—anon:
There's joy on the mountains;
There's life in the fountains;
Small clouds are sailing,
Blue sky prevailing;
The rain is over and gone!

(William Wordsworth)

译文

进行曲

公鸡在啼叫,
清溪在流淌,

小鸟唧唧喳喳,
湖泊闪着光,
绿野晒着太阳。
老人和孩子
与壮年人一起工作。
牛儿在吃草,
从不抬起头。
虽有四十头,却似一头样!

犹如一支战败的军队,
在光秃秃的山坡上,
雪已悄然融退,
这阵更是惨败。
耕童时时在田垄呼喊,
笑声充满大山,
伴着生机勃勃的喷泉;
浮云悠悠飘过,
蓝天渐渐显现;
正是雨过天晴!

(威廉·华兹华斯)

作者介绍

威廉·华兹华斯非常热爱乡村,在英国的湖区度过了大半生。《露西》《她在阳光雨露中成长的三年》《黄水仙》《露西·格雷》《诗人的船》和《我们七岁》是他创作的一些简短的诗歌。

The Voice of Spring

I am coming, little maiden,
With the pleasant sunshine laden;
With the honey for the bee;
With the blossom for the tree;
With the flower and with the leaf;
Till I come the time is brief.

I am coming, I am coming!
Hark! the little bee is humming;
See! the lark is soaring high,
In the bright and sunny sky,
And the gnats are on the wing:
Little maiden, now is spring.

See the yellow catkins cover,
All the slender willows over;
And on mossy banks so green,
Star-like primroses are seen;
Every little stream is bright;
All the orchard trees are white.

Hark the little lambs are bleating,
And the cawing rooks are meeting,
In the elms—a noisy crowd;
And all birds are singing loud;
And the first white butterfly,
In the sun goes flitting by.

Turn thy eyes to earth and heaven:
God for thee the spring has given,

Taught the birds their melodies,
Clothed the earth and cleared the skies,
For thy pleasure or thy food—
Pour thy soul in gratitude.

(Mary Howitt)

译文

春之声

我来了，娇小的姑娘，
满载着喜悦的阳光；
给蜜蜂送来甜蜜，
为枝头披上花衣；
带来鲜花带来绿叶；
我来了，我很快就来到。

我来了，我来了！
听！小蜜蜂"嗡嗡"叫；
看！云雀也飞得高，
在晴朗灿烂的天空下，
小昆虫飞来飞去多逍遥。
春天来了，娇小的姑娘。

看哪！嫩黄的柔叶爬出枝头，
将所有柔嫩的杨柳儿覆盖；
长满苔藓的河岸绿意莹然，
报春花星星点点映入眼帘；
每一条小溪都波光闪闪；
雪白的花朵把所有果树开遍。

听哪！小羊羔在"咩咩"叫，
白嘴鸦在"呱呱"叫，
相会在榆树林——一大群吵吵闹闹；
鸟儿都在放声歌唱；
第一只白蝴蝶掠过，
沐浴着灿烂的阳光。

低头看大地，抬头看天；
上帝把春天送到你身边，
教会鸟儿美妙的乐曲，
装扮好大地，又把天空擦净，
送给你快乐，送给你食物——
所以，请对造物主心存感恩。

（玛丽·豪伊特）

♪ 作者介绍

豪伊特夫人是英国人，非常喜爱孩子，并为他们创作了许多作品。她是第一个把安徒生的童话大量翻译成英文的人。

Ho! For the Bending Sheaves

Ho! for the bending sheaves,
Ho! for the crimson leaves
Flaming in splendor!
Season of ripened gold,
Plenty in crib and fold,
Skies with depth untold,
Liquid and tender.

Autumn is here again,
Banners on hill and plain,
Blazing and flying,
Hail to the amber morn,
Hail to the heaped up corn.
Hail to the hunter's horn,
Swelling and dying!

(James Russell Lowell)

译文

噢！压弯的庄稼捆

噢！压弯的庄稼捆，
噢！绯红的树叶，
像燃烧的火焰般灿烂夺目！
在金秋，收获的季节，
谷仓充实，羊儿成群，
苍穹深邃无尽，
清澈又温柔。

秋天又来了,
岬角和平原上的旗帜,
鲜艳光彩,迎风飘扬,
向琥珀色的晨曦问好,
向高耸的谷堆致意。
向捕猎者的号角致敬,
响亮高亢,直至平息!

(詹姆斯·罗素·洛厄尔)

♪ 作者介绍

詹姆斯·罗素·洛厄尔,散文家、诗人。他住在马萨诸塞州。其佳作有《噢!压弯的庄稼捆》《蒲公英》《初雪》《源泉》《被偷换的孩子》《朗福尔爵士的愿景》等。

Chapter 4
Stories of Animal Life | 动物的生活

预习

bribe /braɪb/ 贿赂
earnest /ˈɜːrnɪst/ 诚挚
measure /ˈmeʒər/ 方法
mosquito /məˈskiːtoʊ/ 蚊子
particular /pərˈtɪkjələr/ 特别的
passenger /ˈpæsɪndʒər/ 乘客
respect /rɪˈspekt/ 方面
trial /ˈtraɪəl/ 考验

Little Mitchell

Baby Mitchell was an August squirrel. That is, he was born in the month of August.

His pretty gray mother found a nice hole, high up in the crotch of a tall chestnut tree, for her baby's nest. Then she lined it with soft fur plucked from her own loving little breast, for that is the way the squirrel mothers do.

This chestnut tree grew in a great forest on the side of a steep mountain, named Mount Mitchell. This is the highest mountain peak in all the eastern half of the United States. It is in North Carolina, where there are many beautiful mountains, and is one of the most beautiful of them all.

One night the little gray bunny mother did not come home, and the baby in the old chestnut tree became hungry and cried all night. No doubt he was cold, too, for he had no little furry mother to curl herself about him and keep him warm.

Little Mitchell was only two or three days old, and did not have his eyes open, yet when morning came, he felt so bad, that he climbed up to the crotch of the tree to find out what he could. Then he tried to walk out into space, and down he fell.

He caught at the tree-trunk with his little claws, and in that way managed to get hold of a piece of loose bark. There he clung, frightened, and crying like a baby-which, indeed, he was.

Then a lady, who was climbing to the top of Mount Mitchell, came along, found the baby squirrel, and rescued him. She took him with her, and, although she was on a journey, she gave him the best of care.

She used to give him warm milk out of a spoon three or four times a day. Every day he took a little more, and every day he grew a little larger.

When he was older, she one day brought him some chestnuts. They were the very first to get ripe. She did not give them to Little Mitchell until she had roasted them in the hot ashes, and made them quite soft.

Then she gave him one, and the baby took it in his hands, sat up as well as he could, and looked very wise indeed.

But he was just making believe, for he did not know in the least what to do with that nut.

He sniffed at it, but seemed to have no idea what was inside, until the lady opened it for him. Then he ate a piece of it, gnawing it with his four little front teeth, and liked it very much.

Every day after that he had roasted chestnuts with his milk. Soon he learned to know them with the shell on, and to take it off. He would bite it loose, and then give it a fling that sent it ever so far.

As they traveled on, they came to the chincapin country, and stopped to gather some chincapins, for they were ripe. What are chincapins? Why, don't you know? All the children that live in the South know what chincapins are. They are not berries! No, guess again.

Yes, nuts; little shiny brown nuts, like baby chestnuts. The mountain children often string them for beads, because they are so pretty.

The chincapins grow in little burrs, like tiny chestnut burrs; but there is only one nut in a burr instead of two or three, and they grow on bushes or little trees, with leaves like chestnut leaves, only smaller.

Mitchell liked the nuts, which are very sweet, and he could crack them for himself, because the shells are soft, like chestnut shells. So he sat on the lady's knee in the chincapin patch, and cracked chincapins. When he had succeeded in getting a shell off, he would give it a toss that sent it far away.

Once when Little Mitchell had grown to be quite a squirrel, the lady thought that perhaps he was old enough to take care of himself, and would like to be set free in the woods. That, you know, is the best home for the little squirrel folk.

When he had finished his dinner of chestnuts that day, the lady put him down on the ground near a little tree. Then she went back to the place where she had been sitting, and left him.

Little Mitchell first looked around at the big, wild lonely forest, and then at his dear lady. As soon as he could think, he ran and scrambled and scampered as fast as his legs could carry him-not up the tree, oh, no, indeed!——But straight back to his lady.

He climbed into her lap, stuck his head up her sleeve, and seemed glad to be with her again. She then made up her mind to take care of him, and when she went to her home in the North, Little Mitchell went with her and lived with her.

(Margaret Warner Morley)

译文

小松鼠米切尔

小松鼠米切尔是只八月的松鼠，也就是说，他出生在八月。

松鼠妈妈有着一身美丽的灰色皮毛，她在高高的栗子树上找了一个舒服的树洞，当作母子两人的新家。她还从自己小小的胸膛上拔下许多软毛垫在窝里，每一位松鼠妈妈都是这么做的。

这棵栗子树长在米切尔山的大森林里。米切尔山非常陡峭，是美国东部地区最高的山。北卡罗来纳州群山绵延，这座山是其中最美丽的一座。

一天晚上，可爱的灰松鼠妈妈没能回家，松鼠宝宝被独自留在了树洞里。没有妈妈为他送来美味的食物，也没有妈妈蜷缩着身体为他御寒，松鼠宝宝饥寒交加，一整夜都在放声大哭。

可怜的小米切尔只有两三天大，就连眼睛都还没有睁开。到了第二天早上，他的状态愈加糟糕。他想爬到树杈上去找点儿什么。他刚刚走出家门，就从树上摔了下来。

幸好他用小爪子抓住了树干上一块松散的树皮，他害怕地紧紧抱着那块树皮，像个宝宝一样哭了起来。他的确还是个小宝宝啊。

这时，一位正在爬山的女士看到了挂在半空的松鼠宝宝，于是将他救了下来。虽然这位女士还在旅行，但她还是将小松鼠带在了身边，竭尽所能地照顾着他。

一天里她会给小松鼠喂三四次温牛奶。随着每天进食量的增加，小松鼠也在不断地长大。

当他长大一点儿的时候，这位女士给了他一些栗子。这些栗子已经成熟了，但她仍然细心地把栗子在炭火上烤了一会儿，烤得又软又糯之后才会给米切尔。

当她给小松鼠一颗烤过的栗子，小松鼠双手接过栗子后端端正正地坐着，看上去很是聪明。

不过这只是表象罢了，事实上他根本不知道该拿这颗坚果怎么办。

他抽着小鼻子使劲儿嗅，但并没有嗅出来果壳里藏的是什么东西。于是，好心的女士只好帮他剥开了果壳。他小心地啃了一口，用那四颗小前牙嚼个不停，看上去十分喜欢吃。

从那之后，米切尔每天都能配着牛奶吃上几颗烤过的栗子。过了不久，他认识了带壳的栗子，还学会了怎么把壳给剥掉。他会先将栗子壳咬松，然后猛地一丢，栗子总会被他丢得老远。

这位女士仍在继续旅行，他们来到了一个叫"钦阔平"的地方（chinquapin，谐音"钦阔平"，是一种叫毛枝栗的栗子，也是美国的一处地名。），收集了一些成熟的毛枝栗。怎么，你不知道毛枝栗是什么吗？每一个生活在美国南方的孩子都知道毛枝栗是什么。不，它们不是浆果！再猜！

没错，它们是一种小小的、表面光滑的棕色坚果，有点儿像小个儿的栗子，看起来非常漂亮，山里的孩子经常把它们串起来戴在手上或是挂在身上。

这种小坚果生长在类似于栗子的那种毛刺球里。普通栗子一个毛刺球里会长两到三颗栗子，而这种坚果的毛刺球里只会长出一颗果实。这种坚果长在灌木或是小树苗上，叶子要比栗树小上一圈。

米切尔很喜欢这种味道甜美、表皮柔软的坚果，他能自己轻松地剥掉果皮，品尝美味。瞧，在一块长满小坚果的地方，他正坐在好心女士的膝盖上，认认真真剥着坚果皮。每当他剥掉一块果皮，就会将这块果皮扔得远远的。

小松鼠米切尔长成大松鼠之后，这位好心的女士觉得他已经能够自力更生了，也许想要回到自由自在的树林里生活。对于小松鼠来说，显然大自然才是他们最好的家。

那天晚上，等米切尔吃过最爱的栗子，这位女士把他放到一棵小树旁的地上，接着她自顾自地离开了，回到她一开始坐着的地方。

小米切尔看了看广袤孤独的原始森林，又看了看那位亲爱的女士。他连跑带爬，慌慌张张地用最快的速度冲向她。哦，是的，他没往树上爬，而是直接回到了好心女士的身边。

他爬上她的膝头，将头埋在她的袖子里，能又回到她身边，他觉得很高兴。于是，这位女士下定决心要一直照顾这只小松鼠。后来，米切尔跟着她回到了北方的家，和她生活在一起。

（玛格丽特·华纳·莫莉）

✎ 作者介绍

想要知道小松鼠米切尔后来受到的训练以及它的冒险故事，请看《一只山地松鼠的故事》，该书由 A. C. 麦克克勒格公司出版。作者莫莉女士出生于美国艾奥瓦州，著有《生命之歌》《养蜂人》《小蜜蜂》《种子》《胡蜂和它们的生活方式》等精彩书籍。

The Envious Wren

On the ground lived a Hen,
In a tree lived a Wren,
Who picked up her food here and there;
While Biddy had wheat,
And all nice things to eat,
Said the Wren, "I declare, it isn't fair!"

"Now, there is that Hen,"
Said this cross little Wren,
"She's fed till she's fat as a drum;
While I strive and sweat,
For each bug that I get,
And nobody gives me a crumb.

"I can't see for my life,
Why the old farmer's wife,
Treats her so much better than me.
Suppose on the ground,
I hop carelessly round,
For awhile, and just see what I'll see."

So down flew the Wren;
"Stop to tea," said the Hen;
And soon Biddy's supper was sent;
But scarce stopping to taste,
The poor bird left in haste,
And this was the reason she went:

When the farmer's kind dame,

To the poultry yard came,
She said—and the wren shook with fright—
"Biddy's so fat, she'll do
For a pie or a stew,
And I guess I shall kill her to-night."

(Phoebe Cary)

译文

妒忌的鹪鹩

地上生活着一只母鸡,
树上生活着一只鹪鹩。
鹪鹩到处寻找她的食物,
母鸡却有麦粒吃,
以及一切好东西。
鹪鹩说:"我声明,这不公平!"

"瞧,那儿有只母鸡。"
这只痛苦的小鹪鹩说道,
"她被喂得像一面鼓那么胖;
我却为了捕捉每一条虫子,
努力奋斗、汗流浃背,
甚至没人给我一粒面包屑。

"我一辈子都没看明白,
为什么老农夫的妻子
对她比对我好那么多。
不如我到地面上,
随意蹦跳一会儿,

看我会看到什么。"

于是鹪鹩飞下来。
母鸡说:"停下来喝杯茶。"
很快母鸡的晚餐被送来,
但鹪鹩没有停下来品尝,
可怜的鸟儿迫不及待地离开,
下面我们会说她离开的理由。

当农夫好心的妻子
来到饲养家禽的院子,
她说——鹪鹩吓得直抖——
"母鸡真肥,可以用她
做馅饼或是炖汤,
我想今晚我要杀掉她。"

(菲比·加里)

Catching Charlie

This morning, while the dew was yet on the grass, word came that Charlie had got away. Now Charlie is a most important member of the family, and as shrewd a horse as ever need be.

Lately he had found out the difference between being harnessed by a boy and by a man. So it has happened several times, that as soon as the halter dropped from his head, before the bridle could take its place, Charlie backed boldly out of the stable, in spite of the stout boy pulling with all his might at his mane and ears.

On this particular morning, we were to put a passenger friend on board the cars at ten minutes past eight o'clock; it was now thirty minutes past seven. Out popped Charlie from his stall, like a cork from a bottle, and lo! some fifty acres there were in which to try his legs and ours, to say nothing of tempers.

First, the lady with a measure of oats attempted to do the thing by bribing him. Not he! He had no objection to the oats, none to the hand, until it came near his head; then off he sprang.

After one or two trials, we dropped the oats, and went at it in good earnest,——called all the boys, headed him off this way, ran him out of the growing oats, drove him into the upper lot, and out of it again.

We got him into a corner with great pains, and he got himself out of it without the least trouble. He would dash through a line of six or eight whooping boys with as little effort as if they had been so many mosquitoes.

Down he ran to the lower side of the lot, and down we all walked after him. Up he ran to the upper end of the lot, and up we all walked after him—too tired to run.

Oh, it was glorious fun——to him! The sun was hot, the train were coming, and we had two miles to drive to the depot. He did enjoy it, and we did not.

We tried a new plan——opened wide the great gate of the barn-yard, and attempted to drive him in; and we did it, too——almost; for he ran close up to it——and just sailed past, with a laugh as plain on his face as ever horse had.

A man is away ahead of a horse in many respects ; but running on a summer day, in a twenty-acre lot, is not one of them. We got him by the brook, and while he drank——oh, how slowly!——we started up and succeeded in just missing our grab at his mane.

Now comes another splendid run. His head is up, his eyes flashing, his tail streaming out like a banner. Glancing his head this way and that, right and left, he allows us to come into the brush corner, from whence, in a few moments, he allows us to come out, and again follow him down to the barn.

But luck will not hold forever, even with horses. He dashed down a lane, and we had him. But as soon as he saw the gate closed, and understood the state of the case, how charmingly he behaved! He allowed us to come up and bridle him without a movement of resistance. He also showed by his whole conduct that it was the merest sport in the world, this seeming wrong-doing; and to him we have no doubt it was.

(Henry Ward Beecher)

译文

捉住查理

这天早晨,晨露未晞的时候,就有消息传来,说查理跑了。查理是一匹马,我们爱极了他,把他当家人看待。只不过,他机灵得有点过头了。

最近,他发现,同样是上马具,男孩和男人就不一样。他开始多次捣蛋。瞧,缰绳刚从他的头上落下,马鞍还没固定好,查理就猛地退出了马厩,那个胖小子不管怎么使劲揪他的鬃毛和耳朵,对他可一点用都没有。

在这个特殊的早上,我们本来打算送一位顾客朋友上八点十分的车。那时是七点半,查理"砰"的一声从栏位里跳出来,就跟冲出酒瓶的软木塞似的。接下来你就看着吧！他开始在二十公顷的地上疯跑，考验他自己的蹄子和我们的脚丫子，还考验我们的脾气。

一开始，有的女士妄图使用贿赂燕麦的策略。这招不灵！他不会和燕麦过不去，也不讨厌你伸过去的手，但等你要靠近他的头部时，他就跳开了。

一两次失败之后，我们放弃了"燕麦策略"，开始动真格的——叫上所有男孩，拦他，把他从燕麦地里赶出去，逼到最高处，然后再把他赶下来。

我们把他逼到一个角落要费上好大力气，但他从角落出来却轻而易举。他飞奔着，穿过六七八个大呼小叫地想把他赶回去的男孩，动作轻松之极，仿佛他们不过是一群蚊子。

他往地势较低的那头跑，我们就跟在他后面走下去；他往地势较高的那头跑，我们又跟在他后面走上来——我们已经累得跑不动了。

啊，这真是有意思极了——对他自己而言。阳光热辣辣的，车就要到站了，我们还要乘马车赶到三千米外的停车场。他还没玩够呢，我们就不一样了。

我们又尝试新办法——把畜棚围栏的大栅栏门敞开，想把他赶进去。我们做到了——几乎做到了——他离栅栏门近了，更近了——然后一掠而过，在那张马脸上竟然露出嘲笑的表情。

在许多方面，人都是远远超过马的；但大夏天狂奔在八公顷的马场上，就不是人类的强项了。我们在小溪那里撵上了他，趁他在饮水的时候——哼，他的速度也不过如此！——我们突然出动，然后成功地与他的鬃毛失之交臂。

于是，精彩的追逐戏还要继续。他头颅高高抬起，双眼闪着精光，尾巴如旗帜般飘扬，他一会儿转头奔向这里，一会儿转头奔向那里，左一下，右一下，他把我们引到角落，转眼又把我们引出来，带到畜棚那边。

然而谁也不会一直走运，马也是一样。他沿着一条小道猛跑的时候，我们抓到了他。他一看到栅栏门关上，就明白了自己的处境。他规规矩矩的样子真是迷人！他刚才让我们都来抓他，我们也只得照做。他觉得自己不过是找了点乐子，根本算不上犯了什么错——从他的所作所为来看，毫无疑问他就是这么认为的。

（亨利·沃德·比彻）

Arnaux, Homing Pigeon

The hardest of all work for a Homing Pigeon is overseas, for there is no chance of aid from landmarks. The hardest of all times for him at sea is a fog, for then even the sun is blotted out, and there is nothing whatever to guide him.

With memory, sight, and sound all gone, the Homer has one thing left, and herein is his great strength: the inborn sense of direction. There is only one thing that can destroy this, and that is fear, hence the necessity of a stout little heart between those noble wings.

Arnaux, Starbock, and Cornerbox, in a course of training, had been shipped on an ocean steamer bound for Europe. They were nearly a year old, and had already had several months of training on land.

Now they were to be tested at sea. They were to be set free out of sight of land, but a heavy fog set in and forbade their start. The steamer took them on, intending to send them back on the next vessel.

When ten hours out, the engine broke down, the fog settled dense over the sea, and the vessel was adrift and helpless as a log. She could only whistle for assistance, but that was really of no use. Then the pigeons were thought of.

Starbock was first selected. A message for help was written on waterproof paper, rolled up, and lashed to his tail-feathers on the under side. He was thrown into the air and disappeared.

Half an hour later Cornerbox was laden with a message. He flew up, but almost immediately he returned, and alighted on the rigging. He was the picture of Pigeon fear; nothing would induce him to leave the ship. He was so frightened, that he was easily caught and thrust back into the coop.

Now the third was brought out——a small, chunky bird. The shipmen did not know him, but they noted down from his anklet his name and number——Arnaux, 2590 C. It meant nothing to them, but the officer that held him noticed that his heart did not beat so wildly as that of the last bird had done.

The message was taken from Cornerbox. It ran——Ten A.M. Tuesday. We broke our shaft two hundred ten miles out from New York; we are drifting helplessly in the fog. Send out a tug as soon as possible. We are whistling one long, followed by one short, every sixty seconds. (Signed) THE CAPTAIN.

This was rolled up, wrapped in waterproof film, addressed to the steamship company, and lashed to the under side of Arnaux's middle tail-feather.

When thrown into the air, he circled around the ship, then around again higher and higher, then again higher in a wider circle, and he was lost to view. Still higher he went till quite out of sight and feeling of the ship and above the fog.

Shut out now from the use of all his senses but one, he gave himself up to that. Strong in him that was, and there was no room for the tyrant Fear.

True as a needle to the pole went Arnaux now, no hesitation, no doubts. Within one minute of leaving the coop, he was speeding straight as a ray of light for the loft where he was born, the only place on earth where he could be made content.

That afternoon Billy was on duty at the pigeon loft when the whistle of fast wings was heard. A blue flyer flashed into the loft, and made for the water-trough.

He was gulping down mouthful after mouthful when Billy gasped:"Why, Arnaux, it's you-you beauty." Then, with the quick habit of the Pigeon man, he pulled out his watch and marked the time, 2:40 P.M.

A glance showed the tie-string on the tail. Billy shut the door, and dropped the catch-net quickly over Arnaux's head. A minute later he had the roll in his hand; in two minutes he was speeding to the office of the steamship company.

There he learned that Arnaux had made the two hundred and ten miles in fog, over sea, in four hours and forty minutes. Within another hour the needful help had set out for the steamer.

Two hundred miles in fog over sea in four hours and forty minutes. This was a noble record. Cornerbox came back on the tug. Starbock never was heard of again. No doubt he perished at sea.

(Ernest Thompson Seton)

译文

信鸽阿诺斯

对于一只信鸽来说，最难的工作就是飞越海洋，因为他完全没法从地标中获得帮助。而在海洋上空最难的是遇上大雾的时候。那时，太阳被浓雾遮蔽，再没有什么能够为他指明方向了。

记忆、视觉和听觉相继丧失，信鸽只剩下一样东西，这也正是他强大力量的所在，那就是与生俱来的方向感。除非感到恐惧，否则信鸽不会丧失这种方向感，因此他那高洁的翅膀之间必须要有一颗坚定勇敢的心。

一艘驶往欧洲的海洋汽船将还在接受训练的阿诺斯、斯达波克和克纳博克斯送到了海上。他们大约一岁了，已经在陆地上接受了几个月的训练。

现在他们要在海洋上进行测试。按照原计划，他们要在看不见陆地的地方开始飞，但是测试被一场浓雾耽搁了。汽船会载着这些信鸽继续航行，再让下一艘轮船把他们带回来。

十小时后，浓雾笼罩着海面，轮船的引擎坏了，像一根木头一样无助地随波逐流。轮船鸣响汽笛求救，但实际上这毫无用处。这时，船员想到了信鸽。

斯达波克是第一个被选中的。船员在防水纸上写上了一条求救信息，然后卷好这张纸，绑在鸽子的尾羽上。鸽子被扔向天空，然后消失了。

一个半小时以后，克纳博克斯带着一条信息飞上了天空，但几乎立刻就飞了回来，降落在了桅杆上。他的行为很好地诠释了什么是鸽子的恐惧，什么都不能诱使他离开这艘船。他太害怕了，船员轻而易举地捉住他，把他塞回了笼子。

现在第三只鸽子出场了，他又小又矮。船员们并不认识他，但他们记下了他脚环上标记的名字和编号——阿诺斯，2590C。他的名字没有什么特殊含义，但是船长握着他的时候，注意到他的心跳不像刚才的鸽子那样激烈。

船员把求救信从克纳博克斯的尾羽上拿下来。信是这样写的：星期二上午十点，我们在离纽约三百三十八千米开外船轴断了，正在大雾里无助地漂流。请尽快派出一艘救援拖船。我们每隔一分钟鸣一次汽笛，一声长一声短。（签名）船长。

求救信被卷起来裹在防水胶布里，上面写着汽船公司的地址。然后，船员把它绑在了阿诺斯的尾羽下面。

阿诺斯被放飞到空中。他围着船绕圈子，渐渐越飞越高，越飞越远，最后消失在茫茫雾海中。他一直飞到雾的上方，就看不见那艘船了，也感觉不到船的存在。

现在，除了方向感以外他的所有其他感官都失效了。他专注于辨别方向。他的心无比坚定，没给那个名叫"恐惧"的暴君一点机会。

仿佛受到磁铁的吸引一样，阿诺斯毫不犹豫，毫不怀疑。他一离开笼子就朝自己的出生地疾飞过去，就像一束光一样直奔鸽房而去。全世界只有那里，才能让他感到满意。

那天下午，比利正在鸽房值勤时，他听到翅膀快速拍打的声音。一只青色的鸽子飞进了鸽房，冲向了水槽。

他一口接一口地狼吞虎咽，而比利则倒抽了口气："天啊，是你，阿诺斯，你这个美丽的小东西。"然后，出于养鸽人的习惯，他拿出手表记下了时间：下午两点四十分。

比利瞥见了阿诺斯尾巴上系着的绳子，他关上门，用捕捉网飞快地从鸽子头上罩了下去。一分钟以后，他手里拿着那个纸卷；两分钟后他急速跑到了汽船公司的办公室。

在那里，他得知阿诺斯在雾气弥漫的海上飞行了三百三十八千米，飞行时间为四小时四十分钟。接下来，一个小时之内，轮船急需的救援船就出发了。

大雾笼罩的海上，四小时四十分钟，三百三十八千米。这是一个了不起的记录。克纳博克斯跟着拖船回来了，而斯达波克再也没有了消息，毫无疑问他消失在了海洋深处。

（欧内斯特·汤普森·西顿）

Moti Guj(1)

Once upon a time there was a coffee-planter in India who wished to clear some forest land for coffee-planting. When he had cut down all the trees and burned the under-wood, the stumps still remained.

For this work the elephant is often used. He will either push the stump out of the ground with his trunk, or drag it out with ropes.

The planter, therefore, hired elephants by ones and twos and threes, and fell to work.

The very best of all the elephants belonged to the very worst of all the drivers. The elephant's name was Moti Guj, which means the Pearl Elephant. Deesa was the name of his master and driver.

When Deesa had made much money through the strength of his elephant, he would drink, and then give Moti Guj a beating with a tent-peg over the tender nails of the forefeet.

Moti Guj never trampled the life out of Deesa at these times, for he knew that after the beating was over, Deesa would embrace his trunk and weep and call him his love and his life, and give him some liquor. Then Deesa would go to sleep between Moti Guj's forefeet, and the elephant would stand guard over him until his master saw fit to wake up.

There was no sleeping in the daytime on the planter's clearing. The wages were too high to risk. Deesa sat on Moti Guj's neck and gave him orders, while Moti Guj rooted up the stumps——for he owned a magnificent pair of tusks; or pulled at the end of a rope——for he had a magnificent pair of shoulders, while Deesa kicked him behind the ears, and said that he was the king of elephants.

At evening time Moti Guj would wash down his three hundred pounds' weight of green food with a quart of liquor, and Deesa would take a share and sing songs between Moti Guj's legs till it was time to go to bed.

Once a week Deesa led Moti Guj down to the river, and Moti Guj lay on his side in the shallows, while Deesa went over him with a coir-swab and a brick. Afterwards they would come up, Moti Guj all black and shining, waving a torn branch twelve feet long in his trunk, and Deesa knotting up his own long wet hair.

It was a peaceful, well-paid life till Deesa felt the return of the desire to drink deep. Then he went to the planter, and asked permission to go away for ten days.

After Deesa had spoken the truth, the planter said, "I would give you leave to go, Deesa, if anything could be done with Moti Guj while you are away. You know that he will obey only your orders."

"May I call up Moti Guj?" asked Deesa.

Permission was granted, and in answer the lordly tusker swung out of the shade of a clump of trees where he had been squirting dust over himself till his master should return.

"Light of my heart, give ear," said Deesa, standing in front of him. Moti Guj saluted with his trunk.

"I am going away," said Deesa. "I shall be gone for ten days. Hold up your near forefoot, and I'll impress the fact upon it." Deesa took a tent-peg and banged Moti Guj ten times on the nails. Moti Guj grunted and shuffled from foot to foot.

"Ten days." said Deesa. "You must work and haul and root trees as Chihun here shall order you. Take up Chihun and set him on your neck." Moti Guj curled the tip of his trunk, Chihun put his foot there, and Chihun was swung on to the neck. Deesa handed Chihun the heavy iron elephant-goad.

Chihun thumped Moti Guj's bald head. The elephant trumpeted.

"Be still," said Deesa. "Chihun is your master for ten days. Now bid me good-by, beast after mine own heart. Jewel of all elephants, adieu!"

Moti Guj lapped his trunk round Deesa and swung him into the air twice. That was his way of bidding the man good-by.

"He will work for Chihun now," said Deesa to the planter. "Have I leave to go?"

The planter nodded, and Deesa dived into the woods. Moti Guj went back to haul stumps.

(Joseph Rudyard Kipling)

译文

莫蒂·古吉拉特（1）

从前，有位印度的咖啡种植园主想清理掉一片树林来种咖啡。他砍光了所有的树，烧尽了低矮的灌木丛，但树桩还留在那里。

通常这样的活是交给大象的，他会用鼻子将树桩推出地面或用绳索把他拉出来。

于是，种植园主零零散散地雇了几头大象，让他们来干这活儿。

最好的大象恰好属于最坏的驭象人。这头大象的名字叫莫蒂·古吉拉特，也就是"象中明珠"的意思。他的主人名字叫作迪萨，也是他的驭象人。

每当迪萨靠古吉拉特的力气赚到很多钱时，他会去喝酒，还会用帐篷桩子抽打古吉拉特前脚上柔嫩的指甲。

这种时候，古吉拉特也不会想要踩死迪萨，因为他知道抽打结束后，迪萨肯定会抱住他的鼻子，啜泣着叫他"心肝宝贝"，并给他点酒喝。随后迪萨便会在古吉拉特的两只前脚中间进入梦乡，而大象则会在主人醒来前一直守护着他。

整个白天，在种植园主安排的工作时间是不准睡觉的。工资很高，不值得冒风险偷懒。坐在他脖子上的迪萨只要一声令下，古吉拉特就会用那对大大的长牙，或他那有力的肩膀，拉住绳索的一头，将树桩连根拔起。这时，迪萨就会踢踢他的耳朵，称他为象中之王。

晚上，古吉拉特会将一百多千克蔬菜和一升酒一扫而空，而迪萨也会分享属于他自己的那一份，在象腿之间放声歌唱，直到睡去。

每周，迪萨都会把莫蒂·古吉拉特带到河边。大象侧躺在浅滩上，而迪萨则会用椰壳做成的抹布以及一块砖头为他擦身。等他们起身时，莫蒂·古吉拉特全身黝黑，闪闪发亮，他会用鼻子挥舞起一根三十厘米长的断枝，而迪萨则会盘起他那湿答答的长发。

度过一段安宁富裕的日子之后，迪萨觉得他的酒瘾又上来了。他去找了种植园主，请求放十天假。

听了迪萨的真心话，种植园主回答说："迪萨，如果你不在时莫蒂·古吉拉特还能继续干活，我允许你离开。你也知道他可只听你的。"

"我能把莫蒂·古吉拉特叫过来一下吗？"迪萨问道。

请求被允许了，这个长着一对长牙的大家伙从一片树丛的阴影下大摇大摆地走了出来，在主人回到身边之前他一直忙碌着，弄得满身尘土。

"我的小宝贝，听我说。"迪萨站在他跟前说道，莫蒂·古吉拉特则用他的长鼻子行了个礼。

"我要走了，"迪萨说，"我会离开十天。举起你这边的前脚，我要在上面给你留点记性。"迪萨拿起一根帐篷桩子在莫蒂·古吉拉特的指甲上狠狠敲了十次。大象咕噜着，抬起脚来回躲闪。

迪萨说："十天内，你要听治勋的命令，好好干活，拖运大树。举起治勋把他放在你的脖子上。"莫蒂·古吉拉特卷起他的鼻尖，治勋就被摇摇晃晃地放在了象脖上。迪萨把沉重的铁象鞭递给了治勋。

治勋踩了踩莫蒂·古吉拉特光秃秃的头，大象大叫了起来。

"安静点，"迪萨说道，"这十天里治勋是你的主人。我心中的好伙计，现在向我告别吧。象中之宝，再见了！"

莫蒂·古吉拉特用长鼻卷起了迪萨，两次把他举到空中，这是他向主人告别的方式。

"现在他会为治勋工作了，"迪萨对种植园主说，"那我可以走了吧？"

种植园主点头同意，迪萨便一头钻入树林，而莫蒂·古吉拉特也回去拖树桩了。

（约瑟夫·鲁德亚德·吉卜林）

Moti Guj(2)

Chihun was very kind to Moti Guj, but the elephant felt unhappy and forlorn. He wanted Deesa again, the savage beatings and the savage caresses. None the less he worked well, and the planter wondered.

The morning of the eleventh day dawned, and there returned no Deesa. Moti Guj was loosed from his ropes for the daily task. He swung clear, looked around, shrugged his shoulders, and began to walk away, as one having business elsewhere.

"Hi! ho! Come back!" shouted Chihun. "Come back and put me on your neck."

Moti Guj gurgled gently, but did not obey. Chihun ran after him with a rope and caught him up. "None of your nonsense with me," said Chihun.

"Hrrump!" said Moti Guj, and walked off. He strolled about the clearing, making fun of the other elephants, who had just set to work. Chihun reported to the planter, who came out with a whip and cracked it furiously. Moti Guj charged him nearly a quarter of a mile across the clearing, "Hrrumping" him into the veranda.

"We'll thrash him." said the planter.

Two huge elephants were brought and the work given to them. They took big chains with which to beat Moti Guj, but Moti Guj drove them both from the field. That decided the planter to argue no more.

At sundown Moti Guj returned for food. "If you won't work, you shan't eat," said Chihun angrily, "You're a wild elephant. Go back to your jungle."

Chihun's little fat baby, rolling on the floor of the hut, stretched its fat arms toward Moti Guj. The elephant knew well that it was the dearest thing on earth to Chihun. He swung out his trunk with a crook at the end, and a moment afterwards the brown baby was crowing in the air twelve feet above the father's head.

"Great Chief!" said Chihun. "Flour cakes of the best, twelve in number, two feet across, and two hundred pounds' weight of young sugar-cane shall be yours this instant. Deign to put down safely that child who is my heart and my life."

Moti Guj tucked the brown baby comfortably between his forefeet, and waited for his food. He ate it, and the brown baby crawled away. Moti Guj dozed, and thought of Deesa. That night he went in search of Deesa, but did not find him either in the undergrowth or at the river.

At dawn Deesa returned. He drew a long breath when he saw that nothing was injured; for he knew something of Moti Guj's temper.

"Call up your beast," said the planter. Deesa shouted in the elephant language, and Moti Guj came. He fell into Deesa's arms trumpeting with joy, and the man and the beast wept over each other and kissed each other, and handled each other, to see that no harm had befallen.

"Now we will get to work," said Deesa. "Lift me up, my son and my joy."

Moti Guj swung him up, and the two went to the coffee-clearing to look for irksome stumps.

The planter was too astonished to be very angry.

(Joseph Rudyard Kipling)

译文

莫蒂·古吉拉特（2）

治勋对莫蒂·古吉拉特很温柔，但大象却并不高兴，感到很孤独。他想念迪萨，也想念他粗鲁的抽打和照顾。让种植园主惊讶的是，他仍然工作得很好。

第十一天清晨，迪萨还是没有回来。莫蒂·古吉拉特被解下索套，开始了一天的工作。但他来回摇晃着，瞧瞧四周，耸了耸肩就走开了，就好像有别的事一样。

"喂！回来！"治勋大叫，"快回来，把我放在你脖子上。"

莫蒂·古吉拉特温和地咕噜着,但没有听从命令。治勋拿着绳子追赶着将他抓住,说道:"别对我耍花招。"

莫蒂·古吉拉特"嗷"的一声走开了。他在空地上闲逛,和其他刚开始工作的大象开玩笑。治勋向种植园主汇报了这一切,后者拿着一根鞭子走了出来,狠狠地抽打他。莫蒂·古吉拉特在空地上追着他跑了四十千米,"嗷嗷"叫着将他赶入了门廊。

"我们会让他屈服的。"种植园主说道。

这项工作被交给了两头大象,他们带着粗大的锁链来对付莫蒂·古吉拉特,但都被他赶跑了,种植园主也只得作罢。

太阳落山时莫蒂·古吉拉特回来找食吃。"如果你不工作,你就不能吃饭。"治勋愤怒地说,"你是一头野象,回你的丛林去吧。"

治勋那胖乎乎的婴儿正在小屋的地板上打着滚,向莫蒂·古吉拉特伸出了胖胖的手臂。大象清楚地知道,治勋在世上最爱的就是这个婴儿。他把鼻尖打成了一个圈伸了过去,不一会儿,这个棕色皮肤的婴儿就在他父亲头上三米多高的空中啼哭起来。

治勋叫道:"厨师,快拿来十二个最好的糕点,六十厘米大的。还有九十千克鲜嫩的甘蔗也会马上送到。请赏个脸,把那个孩子安全地放下来吧,这可是我的心肝,是我的命根子。"

莫蒂·古吉拉特将棕色的婴儿舒舒服服地送进自己的前腿间,等待着食物。他吃着东西,婴儿也慢慢地爬走了。随后,莫蒂·古吉拉特打了瞌睡,他还在思念着迪萨。那天夜里,他跑出去寻找迪萨,但无论是在矮树丛中还是在河边都找不到他的踪影。

黎明时分迪萨回来了。他看到大象没有毁掉什么东西,才长舒了一口气,他对莫蒂·古吉拉特的脾气还是了解的。

"把你那头野兽叫过来吧。"种植园主说道。迪萨用象语大声喊叫着,莫蒂·古吉拉特跑了出来。他钻进迪萨的臂弯中高兴地叫,人和象相拥而泣,互相亲吻,互相触碰,想确认彼此都没有受到什么伤害。

"现在让我们开始干活吧。"迪萨吩咐道,"我的孩子,我的开心果,把我举起来吧。"

莫蒂·古吉拉特把他摇摇晃晃地拎起来,两人向咖啡清理场地走去,去找那些讨厌的树桩了。

种植园主震惊得都顾不上生气了。

（约瑟夫·鲁德亚德·吉卜林）

☆ 作者介绍

尽管吉卜林先生在印度出生，他却是一个英国人，在英国接受了教育。他游历过世界上很多地方，并写下了很多关于当地的作品。

他的一部分最有趣的故事是写给年轻人看的，比如《丛林之书》《丛林之书续编》《基姆》《勇敢的船长》《如此故事》和《斯托基公司》。《莫蒂·古吉拉特》选自《黑与白》，而《白色的小海豹》则收入了《丛林之书续编》一书。

The White Seal

Kotick was a little baby seal, all head and shoulders, with pale, watery eyes, as tiny seals must be. But there was something about his coat that made his mother look at him very closely.

"Sea Catch," she said at last, "our baby is going to be white."

"There never has been such a thing in the world as a white seal," Sea Catch snorted.

"I can't help that," said Matka. "There is going to be one now." And she sang the love crooning seal-song that all the mother seals sing to their babies:

You mustn't swim till you're six weeks old,
Or your head will be sunk by your heels;
And summer gales and Killer Whales
Are bad for baby seals.
Are bad for baby seals, dear rat,
As bad as bad can be;
But splash and grow strong,
And you can't be wrong,
Child of the Open Sea!

Of course, the little fellow did not understand the words, at first. He paddled and scrambled about by his mother's side, and learned to scuffle out of the way when his father was fighting with another seal, and the two rolled and roared up and down the slippery rocks.

The first thing that Kotick did was to crawl inland. There he met tens of thousands of babies of his own age, and they played together like puppies, went to sleep on the clean sand, and played again.

Little seals can no more swim than little children, but they are unhappy till they learn.

The first time that Kotick went down to the sea, a wave carried him out beyond his depth. His big head sank and his hind flippers flew up exactly as his mother had told him in the song, and if the next wave had not thrown him back he would have been drowned.

After that he learned to lie in the pool, and let the wash of the waves just cover him and lift him up while he paddled, but he always kept his eyes open for the big waves that might hurt.

He was two weeks in learning to use his flippers. All that while he floundered in and out of the water. He coughed and grunted and crawled up the beach, and took cat-naps on the sand, and went back again, until at last he found that he truly belonged to the water.

Then you can imagine the times that he had with his companions, ducking under the rollers; or coming in on top of a comber and landing with a splash and a splutter as the big waves went whirling far up the beach; or standing up on his tail and scratching his head as the old seals did; or playing "I'm the King of the Castle," on slippery, weedy rocks that just stuck out of the wash.

Now and then he would see a thin fin, like a big shark's fin, drifting along close to shore. He knew that this was the Killer Whale, the Grampus, which eats young seals when he can get them. Then Kotick would head for the beach like an arrow, and the fin would jig off slowly, as if it were looking for nothing at all.

Late in October the seals began to leave St. Paul's for the deep sea, by families and tribes. Matka and Kotick set out together across the Pacific.

Matka showed Kotick how to sleep on his back, with his flippers tucked down by his side, and his little nose just out of the water. No cradle is so comfortable as the long, rocking swell of the Pacific.

This was one of very many things that Kotick learned, and he was always learning. Matka taught him how to follow the cod and the halibut along the under sea banks, and wrench the rockling out of his hole among the weeds; how to skirt the wrecks lying a hundred fathoms below water, and dart like a rifle-bullet in at one port-hole and out at another as the fishes ran.

She taught him, too, how to dance on the top of the waves when the lightning was racing all over the sky, and wave his flippers politely to the Stumpy-tailed Albatross and the Man-of-War Hawk as they went down the wind.

She taught him how to jump three or four feet clear of the water, like a dolphin, flippers close to the side and tail curved; to leave the flying fish alone because they are bony; to take the shoulder-piece out of a cod at full speed ten fathoms deep; and never to stop to look at a boat or a ship, but especially a rowboat.

At the end of six months, what Kotick did not know about deep-sea fishing was not worth the knowing. And all that time he never set flipper on dry ground.

(Joseph Rudyard Kipling)

译文

白色小海豹

柯提克是一只小海豹，他的脑袋和肩膀整个都是白色的，还有一双水汪汪的大眼睛，看起来是这个年龄的海豹应有的模样。但他的皮肤格外白皙，他妈妈忍不住仔仔细细地观察起他来。

"西卡奇，"他妈妈最后说道，"我们的孩子可能会是个白色的海豹。"

"说什么鬼话，世界怎么会有白色海豹这种东西。"西卡奇闷声说道。

"恕我不能苟同，"玛特卡说，"我们这儿就要有一个了。"说完她就用好听的嗓音低声吟唱起海豹之歌，这是所有的海豹妈妈都会唱给自己孩子听的一首歌谣：

在满六周前，亲爱的孩子，你可不要去游泳，
你的步子还不够稳，会让你沉溺水底；
而那夏日的狂风，和那吃人的鲸鱼，
也会伤害你，
会伤害你啊，我的宝贝，
这可能会害死你；
但我的宝贝啊，你要快快长大，
长大了宝贝才能什么都不怕，
大海的孩子啊，终会像大海一样强大。

当然啦，我们的小家伙最初还听不懂这些话。他学会了在他妈妈旁边攀爬戏水，学会了在他爸爸和其他海豹打架时逃开混战，躲在安全的地方。他

们总是打着打着，就大声吼叫着，从滑溜溜的石头上滚下来。

柯提克做的第一件事就是游到内陆。在这儿，他遇见了数以百万计的跟他差不多大的小海豹，这些小海豹们凑在一起玩耍的样子像极了一群小狗。玩累了，他们就去找干净的沙子睡觉，睡醒了就继续玩。

小海豹的游泳技术不比小孩子强，但他们只要学不会游泳，就会不开心。

柯提克第一次下海的时候，一个浪打过来就把他卷到了深水区。水太深了，他的大脑袋一下子就沉了下去，而他的后蹼一下子就翘了起来，就跟他妈妈在歌谣里唱的一模一样，如果不是又来了一个浪把他打回了沙滩，他可能就会淹死了。

从此以后，他就学会了躺在水浅的地方，让海浪刚好没过他，他则顺势拍打着水面浮上来，但这种时候他总是把眼睛睁得大大的，以防海浪过猛伤到他。

他用两周的时间学会了怎么用他的蹼。不过也就是能在水里翻滚一下的水平。他时常会被呛地咳起来，也会一不小心就"咕噜噜"地灌一口水，然后狼狈地爬回沙滩，在沙滩上打个小盹，醒了再回去继续练，直到最后他才完全熟悉了水性。

这样你就大概能想象到他跟小伙伴们一起玩耍的时候是什么样了，他们经常一猛子扎进浪花底下，或者冲到浪头上，然后等海浪翻涌卷起漩涡时再回到沙滩；或者用尾巴去够脑袋，就像那些成年海豹经常玩的那样；又或者在石头上玩"我是城堡主人"的游戏。那些还沾着海水的石头总是滑溜溜的，杂草丛生。

时不时，他也会看到一些很薄的鳍，朝海滨漂来，看着像是大鲨鱼的鳍。他知道那就是要命的鲸鱼——虎鲸，一种只要抓住小海豹就会吃掉的鲸。这时候，柯提克就会像支利箭一样冲向海滩，而那个鳍则会缓缓离开，仿佛它只是在毫无目的地闲逛。

十月底，海豹们会成群结队地离开圣保罗，前去深海区。玛特卡和柯提克一起出发，他们要穿越太平洋。

玛特卡教会柯提克如何仰泳着睡觉，用前肢在身体两侧划水，只把鼻子露出水面，用来呼吸。柯提克顿时觉得，这世上再没有比太平洋更舒服的摇篮了。

这只是柯提克学会的一个小本事，他总是在学习新技能。玛特卡还教会他，如何跟在鳕鱼或比目鱼后面，照他们的样子在海底游泳，也学会了如何把鳕鱼从它们的洞里赶出来，而这些洞往往藏在海草中间；还学会了如何绕开沉在一百八十多米深的海底的失事船只，在船的一个个窗口中钻来钻去，像个食鱼貂。

除了这些，玛特卡还教会了他当太阳照亮整片天空时，站在浪花顶端跳舞。每次短尾信天翁或鹰队低空飞过时，他还会礼貌地挥舞起自己的鱼鳍来。

她又教柯提克如何一跃就能有一米远，把蹼放在两边，尾巴弯曲，像海豚一样跃过去；不过他们没有学飞鱼，因为飞鱼太瘦了，和柯提克的体型相差太远；她还教他如何还在十八米深的水底像鳕鱼一样飞速前进，并提醒他千万不能停下来看船只，特别是划艇。

等到了月底，柯提克不会的就只剩些无需学习的事情了。此后，他再也不去岸上玩耍了。

（约瑟夫·鲁德亚德·吉卜林）

练习

1.抄写

（1）The hen lived on the ground, and the wren lived in a tree.
　　_____

（2）I envy nobody, and nobody envies me.
　　_____

（3）We got Charlie into a corner, and he got himself out of it.
　　_____

（4）I shall bring the fleece, or I shall never come back.
　　_____

（5）The king did not know him, but he turned pale.
　　_____

（6）The brave lad was nearly frozen, but he was still at his post.
　　_____

（7）Then the king commanded, and they brought Daniel.
　　_____

2.哪些词能在复合句中起连接作用？
　　_____

The Whale's Story

"I see you reading often," said the whalebone to Freddy. "I dare say that you know a good deal about us."

"No, I have not read about you yet, and I know only that you are the biggest fish there is," answered Freddy.

The whalebone creaked and shook, as if it were laughing.

"You are wrong there," it said. "We are not fishes at all, though many stupid persons have called us so for a long time.

"We cannot live without air; we have warm, red blood; and we do not lay eggs. So we are not fishes, but we really are the biggest creatures in the sea and out of it.

"Why, some of us are nearly a hundred feet long. Our tails alone are fifteen or twenty feet wide. The biggest of us weigh five hundred thousand pounds, and have the fat, bone, and muscle of a thousand cattle.

"The lower jaw of one of my family made an arch large enough for a man on horseback to ride under easily. My cousins of the sperm family usually yield eighty barrels of oil."

"What monsters you are!" cried Freddy, taking a long breath.

"I was a right whale from Greenland," went on the bone. "The Sperms live in warm places; but to us the torrid zone is like a sea of fire, and we do not pass it. Our cousins do. They go to the East Indies by way of the North Pole."

"I should like to hear what you eat, and how you live?" said Freddy.

"Well, we do not have any teeth——our branch of the family. We live on creatures so small that you could see them only with a microscope. Yes, you may stare, but it is true.

"The roofs of our mouths are made of whalebone, in broad pieces from six to eight feet long. These are placed one against the other, so as to make a big sieve.

"The tongue lies below, like a cushion of white satin. It is big enough to make five barrels of oil itself.

"When we want to feed, we rush through the water. It is full of the little things that we eat, and we catch them in our sieve, spurting the water through two holes in our heads. Then we collect the food with our tongues and swallow it. Though we are so big, our throats are small.

"We roam about in the ocean, leaping and floating, feeding and spouting, flying from our enemies, or fighting bravely to defend our young ones."

"Have you any enemies? I should not think that you could have; you are so large," said Freddy.

"But we have, and many, too, ——three that attack us in the water, and several more that men use against us. The killer, the sword-fish, and the thrasher trouble us at home.

"Then men harpoon us, shoot us, or entrap us. They make us into oil and candles, and stiffening for gowns and umbrellas," said the bone in a tone of scorn.

Freddy laughed at the idea, and asked, "How about candles? I know about oil and umbrellas, but I thought that candles were made of wax."

"I cannot say much on that point. I know only that when a Sperm whale is killed, they make oil out of the fat part. The Sperms have also a sort of cistern in their heads, full of stuff like cream.

"Men cut a hole in the skull and dip it out. They sometimes get sixteen or twenty barrels. This is made into what you call spermaceti candles."

(Louisa MAlcott)

译文

鲸鱼的故事

"我经常看见你读书。"那副鲸鱼骨架对佛雷德说，"我敢说你非常了解我们。"

佛雷德回答说："不，我还没有读过关于你们的内容，我只知道你们是现存的最大的鱼类。"

鲸骨摇摇头，发出一阵"咔咔"的响声，好像它在笑一样。

"你错了。"它说，"我们根本不是鱼类，虽然很长一段时间里，许多愚蠢的人们总是这么称呼我们。

"我们离开空气就无法生存，我们的血液是温暖的、红色的，而且我们不产卵。所以我们不是鱼类，不过我们确实是海洋里和陆地上最大的生物。

"呵呵，我们之中有一些同伴接近三十米长，单单我们的尾巴就有四到六米宽。最大的同伴重达四十五吨，脂肪、骨头和肌肉加起来相当于一千头牛。

"有一种鲸鱼，它们的下颚拱起来能形成很大的空间，一个人骑着马可以从这块地方很轻松地跑过去。我的亲戚抹香鲸家族中，通常每一条鲸鱼都能产出八十桶鲸油。"

佛雷德深吸一口气，大喊道："你们可真是庞然大物啊！"

"我是一条来自格陵兰岛的露脊鲸。"鲸骨继续说，"抹香鲸生活在温暖的水域里，但对我们来说温水地区就像火海一样，我们不会穿过那里。不过我们的亲戚抹香鲸就行，他们可以穿过北极，游到东印度去。"

佛雷德说："我想听听你们吃些什么，还有你们是怎样生存的？"

"好吧，我们族群中的任何一个家族都没有牙齿。我们以海洋中很小的浮游生物为食，你只有用显微镜才能看见它们。没错，你可能会惊讶地瞪大眼睛，但这都是事实。

"我们嘴巴的顶部由鲸须组成。它们有一两米长，是宽宽的薄片。这些薄片相对排列，形成了一个很大的滤网。

"我们的舌头位于滤网下面，就像一块光滑的白色垫子。我们的舌头非常大，能产出五桶鲸油。

"当我们想要进食的时候，我们就快速从水里穿过。水里到处都是我们吃的浮游生物，我们用滤网把它们抓住，同时把水从头上的两个洞里排出去。然后我们就可以用舌头卷起食物往下吞了。虽然我们很大，但我们的喉咙却很小。

"我们在海洋里漫游、跳跃、浮潜、进食、喷水，当然也得躲避我们的天敌，或者勇敢地为保护下一代而战斗。"

佛雷德说："你们竟然有天敌？我以为你们没有天敌呢，毕竟你们个头这么大。"

"但是我们确实有天敌,而且数量还不少——有三种敌人在水中攻击我们,人类还用好几种武器来对付我们。剑鱼和长尾鲨是我们的天敌,它们给我们带来了许多麻烦。"

鲸骨用一种讥讽的语气说道:"还有,人类用鱼叉戳我们,用枪射击我们,还用陷阱诱捕我们。他们把我们制成鲸油和蜡烛,用我们的骨头来绷紧袍子和雨伞。"

佛雷德笑了起来,问:"蜡烛是怎么回事?我知道鲸油和雨伞,但我以为蜡烛是用蜡做的。"

"在这一点上我也说不太清楚,我只知道他们杀死一条抹香鲸之后,就会用它的脂肪来制油。抹香鲸的头里还有一个大箱子,里面装满了类似奶油一样的东西。

"人类会在我们的头骨上钻一个洞,然后把这些东西挖出来。有时候,他们能挖到十六到二十桶之多。你们所谓的鲸油蜡烛就是用这些东西做的。"

(路易莎·M.奥尔科特)

♪ 作者介绍

奥尔科特女士把自己的早年生活写在了《小妇人》一书中,因此,想要了解她,最好就是读读这本书。奥尔科特女士出生于宾夕法尼亚州,不过她在马萨诸塞州度过了大半生。

本文选自《丁香花下》。该作者还著有《小男人》《传统女孩》《八个堂兄弟》《盛开的玫瑰》和《杰克和吉尔》。

Chspter 5
Fairy Tales | 童话故事

预习

calendar /ˈkælɪndər/ 日历
cordial /ˈkɔːrdʒəl/ 热忱的
creditor /ˈkredɪtər/ 债权人
debtor /ˈdetər/ 债务人
delicate /ˈdelɪkət/ 微妙的
marriage /ˈmærɪdʒ/ 婚姻
protest /ˈproʊtest/ 抗议
whirligig /ˈwɜːrlɪɡɪɡ/ 陀螺

Quackalina

Quackalina, as the old duck at the farm was called, was having trouble. This trouble may be said to have begun in her nest.

In the first place, the farmer's boy had kept her sitting on eggs down to ten by taking one out every day. Then he chose to take her ten beautiful eggs and put them under the guinea-hen, while he fetched the sitting of twenty guinea eggs for Quackalina to hatch.

When the eggs were hatched, Quackalina knew that the first glance into the nest must bring her sorrow. At last the moment came, and she really looked down into the nest. Then it was at least a relief to her to find the nest full of beautiful feathered things.

Little guineas are beautiful, and Quackalina could not help a feeling of pleasure and pride, when she presently found herself crossing the yard, with her twenty dainty, red-booted children.

It was quite in order, to be sure, that she should hurry to the pond with her brood. Would she not have taken her own ducklings there? When she reached the pond, she flapped her tired wings three times for pure gladness at the sight of the beautiful water.

Plunging in, Quackalina took one delightful dive before she turned to the shore. Then in the sweetest tones she invited the little ones to follow her.

But they ——well, they just looked down at their red satin boots and shook their heads. Then it was that Quackalina noticed their feet, and saw that they could never swim.

So she waddled out on the grassy bank, and began to feed them. She gave them some tadpoles, a few blue-bottle flies, and a snail, and several other choice bits, which the guineas seemed to enjoy as much as if they had been young ducks.

When Quackaliua saw that they were quite happy, she started for the very middle of the pond. Oh, how sweet the water was! And now——and now ——and now—— as she dived and dipped and plunged——how it cheered and comforted her heart!

And now comes the glad part of the story. At last Quackalina, turning, said to herself, "I must go ashore now and look after my step-children." She raised her eyes and looked before her to see just where she was.

Then she seemed to see something that was strange and beautiful. Right before her, on the water, swimming easily on its surface, were ten little ugly, smoky, "beautiful" ducks! Ten little ducks that looked just like every one of Quackalina's relations! Now they saw her and began swimming towards her.

Before she knew it, Quackalina had flapped her great wings and quacked aloud three times and three times again!

In less time than it takes to tell it, her own ten beautiful ducks were close about her, and she was kissing every one with her red bill. Then she saw that upon the bank a frightened guinea-hen was tearing along, screeching with terror.

If Quackalina had looked a second time, she would have seen that something beautiful was happening on the bank. At the first note of the guinea's voice, twenty little voices had answered. In a twinkling twenty pairs of red satin boots were running as fast as they could go to meet the great speckled mother-hen.

Soon the whole delighted guinea family was having a happy time away off in the cornfield out of sight and hearing, but Quackalina and her ten little ducklings stayed out on the water nearly all day.

(Ruth McEnery Stuart)

译文

鸭妈妈丽娜

人们习惯把农场里的那只老鸭子叫作鸭妈妈丽娜。她在窝里的时候感到非常苦恼。

一开始,农夫的儿子让她孵十只蛋,想要每天拿走一只破壳的小鸭。但是后来他直接拿走了她漂亮的十只蛋,把他们放到了一只珍珠鸡肚子下面,接着又从珍珠鸡那里拿了二十只鸡蛋给鸭妈妈丽娜孵化。

当这些小鸡破壳的时候,鸭妈妈非常难过,她甚至都不敢朝窝里看一眼。最后,她终于还是低头瞧了瞧,这才松了口气,因为确实有一群美丽的毛茸茸的小生灵挤在窝里。

珍珠鸡幼仔们全都非常漂亮。当鸭妈妈丽娜带着这二十只俊俏的、长着红色脚爪的孩子们穿过院子时,她禁不住从心底感到高兴和骄傲。

她带着一窝孩子急匆匆地赶向池塘,但队伍无疑还算是井然有序。她本来不是打算带着自己的小鸭子们去那儿的吗?他们来到池塘,鸭妈妈丽娜看到美丽的水面,拍打了三下疲惫的翅膀,一股纯粹的喜悦涌上心头。

扑通一声,鸭妈妈丽娜扎入水中,心情舒畅地钻到水下,然后又浮出水面,游向岸边,用最甜蜜的声音招呼小家伙们和她一起玩水。

但是他们……好吧,他们低头看了一下自己光滑的红色脚爪,摇了摇头。这时候鸭妈妈才注意到他们的脚,立刻明白了他们永远没法游泳。

于是她摇摇摆摆地走到绿草如茵的岸边,开始给他们喂食。她喂他们吃了些蝌蚪、肉蝇以及一只蜗牛,还有其他一些美味。小珍珠鸡们和小鸭子们一样,吃得津津有味。

看到小家伙们非常开心，鸭妈妈放心了，她开始向池塘中心游去。哦，水里真是太棒了！此时此刻，她潜入水底，又浮出水面，在水里扑腾，真是既兴奋又舒爽呀！

我们就要讲到最令人高兴的部分了。最后，鸭妈妈丽娜转过身，自言自语道："我现在必须得回岸上去照顾我的养子们。"她抬起眼睛，想看清自己的方位。

然后她似乎看到了什么奇特又美好的事情。就在她前方的水面上，十只丑丑的、灰蒙蒙的、如假包换的小鸭子正在毫不费力地游着。每一只都长得和鸭妈妈丽娜一样！现在，他们看见她了，就朝她游了过来。

鸭妈妈丽娜还没回过神来，只是高兴地拍打着她的大翅膀，"嘎嘎"地叫了又叫！

很快，十只可爱的小鸭子就已经围拢在她身边，她满怀爱意，用红色的嘴巴亲吻每一只小可爱。过了一会儿，她看见岸上有一只珍珠鸡哭个不停，还激动地尖叫着。

如果鸭妈妈丽娜再仔细看看，她就会看见岸上曾上演的动人一幕。一听见珍珠鸡的声音，二十只小鸡就一齐用细弱的嗓音应和起来。眨眼间，二十对红色的光滑小脚"啪嗒啪嗒"飞快地跑向他们有着美丽斑点的母亲。

一会儿之后，幸福的珍珠鸡一家就离开岸边去了玉米地，他们在地里玩得开心极了。虽然看不见他们的身影，但能听见他们叽叽喳喳的声音。而鸭妈妈则几乎一整天都和她的十只小鸭子待在池塘里。

（露丝·麦克内利·斯图尔特）

✿ 作者介绍

露丝·麦克内利·斯图尔特出生于路易斯安那州，在那生活了多年，后来住在纽约市。

斯图尔特女士写了许多故事，她写得最好的几个故事都和孩子有关，比如《巴贝特》和《乔治·华盛顿·琼斯》。这篇《鸭妈妈丽娜》选自故事集《所罗门乌鸦的圣诞口袋》，该书原版由哈柏兄弟出版公司出版。

The Image and the Treasure

In the city of Rome was a graven image of a man. It stood upright, and held out its hand. On the middle finger of the hand were the words "Strike here." No one knew what this meant, but all thought that the image held some hidden treasure.

So the image was marred by blows where one person and another had struck it to find the opening.

At last a learned man looked hard at the image to see if he could find out the secret. The sun was shining brightly. It was noon, and the shadow of the image lay upon the ground. The hand of the shadow was stretched out, and the learned man saw the shadow finger.

He marked the spot, where the tip of the finger rested, and at night, when all was still, he came again. He had brought a spade with him, and he dug down at the spot he had marked.

Soon he came to a trap door. He raised the door, and saw some steps leading down. Then he closed the door above him, and went down the steps.

He found himself in a great hall, and in the middle of the hall was a table. The table was set with dishes of gold and silver, with golden knives and cups of gold.

At one end sat a king and queen. He knew them by their rich robes, and by the crowns on their heads. Fine nobles, too, sat at the table, and all about were men standing.

The wonder was, there was not a sound, and not a single person moved. The king sat still; the queen sat still; the nobles did not stir; the men were fixed. It was as if they were all of stone, and so they were; for when this learned man touched them, he found that they were stone.

He went into a room beyond. There he saw many women dressed in purple. They, too, were of stone. He went into a stable: there stood horses in the stalls, and dogs; but they had all been turned to stone.

So he went about the palace, for palace it plainly was, and everywhere it was as still as death. Not a living thing was to be seen; but there were riches more than he had ever dreamed of.

At last he came back to the great hall. He saw that the light which lighted the hall came from a precious stone in one corner. The light, as he gazed, fell upon a stone archer, who stood with his bow drawn, and the arrow pointed at the precious stone.

On the archer's brow were the words: ——

"I am what I am. My shaft is sure; least of all can the precious stone escape me."

Now the learned man thought to carry away some of the treasures. He went to the table and chose some of the golden cups. They would be the easiest to carry.

But no sooner had he hidden them in his cloak than the arrow sped from the bow and struck the precious stone. In an instant the stone was shivered to bits and there was total darkness.

The learned man groped for the stairs. He could not find them. He went back and forth, but he never found the stairs. He, too, became a stone statue in the secret hall.

(Horace E. Scudder)

译文

雕像与财宝

罗马城里矗立着一座人物雕像。它高高地站着，手掌张开，中指上刻着几个字：就在这里。没人知道这几个字是什么意思，但大家都觉得这座雕像隐藏着某些关于财宝的秘密。

有两个坏蛋甚至用什么东西狠狠击打它，想要找到宝库的入口。因此这座雕像变得满是伤痕。

最终，有一个有学问的人把雕像好好研究了一番，希望能发现其中的秘密。正是中午时分，阳光明亮，雕像的影子映在地上。影子的手掌伸开，这个人注意到了影子的那根手指。

他在那个位置做了个记号。夜晚时分,万籁俱寂,他再次来到这里,还随身带了一把铁锹,在做了记号的地方挖了起来。

不一会儿,他就挖到了一扇紧闭的门。他用力拉起门,看见有台阶通向更深的地方。于是他走进去,关上门,然后顺着台阶向底下走去。

很快他就发现自己来到了一个巨大的大厅里,一张桌子放在大厅的中央。桌子上整齐地摆着金银盘子、金餐刀和金杯子。

国王和王后分别坐在桌子的两头。他能通过他们头上的王冠和身上华贵的长袍认出他们的身份。几名体面的贵族也坐在桌边,其他人都是站着的。

问题是,整个大厅听不到一点儿声音,更没有一个人走动。国王静静坐着,王后静静坐着。贵族们静止不动,其他人也仿佛被固定住似的。他们每一个人都好像石头做的,应该说他们就是石头做的。这个有学问的人摸了摸他们,可以肯定这一点。

他走进旁边一个房间,看见许多穿着紫色衣服的女人。当然,她们也是石头做的。他走进一个马棚,里面有马,还有狗,只可惜它们都变成了石头。

他在宫殿里走来走去,到处是死一般的寂静,看不见一个活物,但到处都是他做梦也想不到的财宝。

最后他还是回到了大厅里,看到一个角落里有一颗闪闪发光的宝石。它发出耀眼的光芒,照亮了整个大厅。他注意到这光芒最终落到了一个石头的弓箭手上。这个弓箭手正张弓搭箭,箭头指着宝石的方向。

弓箭手的前额上刻着这么一段话:

"我就是我。我的箭在弦上,谁也不能从我这里拿走宝石。"

有学问的人想了想,还是决定要带走一些财宝。他走到桌子边,挑选了一些容易携带的金杯子。

他还没来得及把它们藏到外套里,就听见"呼"的一声,那支箭就从弓箭手那里脱手而出,疾冲宝石而去,一击而中。宝石瞬间被击成碎片,黑暗笼罩了整个大厅。

这个人摸索着寻找那些台阶,却找不到。他前前后后地找了好多遍,但再也找不到了那些台阶在哪里了。最后,他也变成了秘密王宫里的一座石头雕像。

(贺拉斯・以利沙・斯卡德)

Little Carl's Christmas

When little Carl was only seven years old, his father and mother died, and he had to go and live with an aunt.

This woman was not kind to him. She kissed him only once a year, and was sorry every time she gave him food. Besides, although she had money, she gave him only very poor clothes.

The poor little fellow was therefore unhappy, and hid himself in out-of-the-way corners to cry when Christmas came. The night before this Christmas the schoolmaster was to take Carl and all the other pupils to church, and bring them back to their homes.

As the weather was cold, and there was a great deal of snow, the children came to the master's house wrapped and bundled up, with fur caps, double jackets, knitted gloves and mittens, and good thick boots.

Only Carl came shivering in the clothes he wore on weekdays and Sundays. On his feet were nothing but coarse stockings and heavy sabots, or wooden shoes.

His thoughtless comrades made a thousand jests over his long face and his poor dress, but Carl tried to take no notice of the boys or what they said. Presently, the troop of boys and their teacher started for the church.

On the way the boys talked of the fine suppers that were waiting them at home. One boy told of a big goose that they were to have.

Another was to have a little fir tree in a wooden box, from whose branches hung oranges, sweetmeats, and toys.

The children spoke, too, of what the Christ-child would bring them, and what He would put into their shoes, which, of course, they would leave in the chimney before going to bed.

Little Carl knew very well that his aunt would send him to bed without any supper, but he had tried all the year to be good and industrious, so he hoped that the Christ-child would not forget him. Therefore, he, too, looked forward to putting his wooden shoes in the ashes of the fireplace.

When the service was ended, the band of children, walking two by two after their teacher, left the church. In the porch, sitting on a stone seat, a child was sleeping——a child clad in a robe of white linen, with bare feet, in spite of the cold.

He was not a beggar, for his robe was new and fresh, and near him on the ground were some carpenter's tools.

Under the light of the stars, his face was sweet, and his golden hair seemed like a crown. But the child's feet were blue in the cold of that December night and were sad to see.

The children so well clothed for the winter passed heedlessly before the unknown child. But little Carl, the last to come out of the church, stopped, full of pity for the sleeping child.

"Alas!" said the orphan to himself, "it is too bad that this little one has to go barefoot in this bad weather. But what is worse than all, he has not even a wooden shoe to leave before him while he sleeps, so that the Christ-child can put something there to comfort him."

Then little Carl took off the wooden shoe from his right foot, and laid it in front of the sleeping child. Limping along on his bare foot, and dragging his stocking through the snow, he followed the boys, and returned to his aunt's house.

"Look at that worthless fellow!" cried his aunt, full of anger when he returned without his right shoe." What have you done with your wooden shoe?"

When the little boy told her what he had done, she burst into a mocking laugh.

"So you take off your shoes for beggars!" she said. "This is something new! Ah, well, since that is so, I am going to put your other shoe in the chimney, and I promise you that the Christ-child will leave there something to-night to whip you with in the morning."

"You shall pass the day tomorrow on dry bread and water," she went on, "we shall see whether the next time you will give away your shoe to the first beggar that comes."

After having given the poor boy a few slaps, his aunt made him climb up to his bed in the attic. The child was grieved to the heart. He went to bed in the dark, and soon went to sleep, his pillows wet with tears.

On the morrow, when the old woman went down stairs, O wonderful sight! She saw the great chimney full of beautiful playthings, and bags of fine candies, and all sorts of good things.

Before all these splendid things stood the left shoe, which she herself had put there that very night, and in which she meant to put a birch rod. By its side stood the right shoe, which her nephew had given to the little waif.

Both were filled with gifts.

As little Carl came running down, and stood before all these beautiful gifts, suddenly there were loud cries and laughter out of doors. The old aunt and little boy went out to see what it all meant. There they found the neighbors gathered together around the fountain in the square.

What had happened? Oh, something very strange and amusing! The children that expected to have only beautiful gifts had found nothing but rods in their shoes.

Then the orphan and the old woman, thinking of all the beautiful things that were in their chimney, were greatly surprised.

Presently they saw the priest coming towards them with wonderment in his face. Then the people understood that in some strange way the beautiful sleeping child, near whom were the carpenter's tools, was the Christ-child.

(François Coppée)

译文

小卡尔的圣诞节

小卡尔只有七岁的时候,他的爸爸妈妈就去世了。他不得不去投靠一位阿姨,和她生活在一起。

这个阿姨对他并不好。她一年才会亲他一次。每次给他食物的时候，她总是格外不高兴。除此之外，她给卡尔穿的衣服都是破破烂烂的，尽管她并不缺钱。

因为这些，可怜的小卡尔总是过得很不开心。每当圣诞节来临的时候，他就躲在不起眼的角落里哭泣。这个圣诞前夜，校长会带着卡尔和学校里的其他同学去教堂，结束之后再送他们回家。

那天，天气非常冷，还下着大雪。孩子们的头上戴着毛皮帽子，身上穿着双层外套，手上还套着针织手套，脚上蹬着厚实的靴子。一个个裹得严严实实，来到了校长的屋子里。

只有卡尔在瑟瑟发抖，他身上的这套衣服，不仅上学时在穿，连周末也在穿。他脚上只穿着一双料子粗劣的袜子，再套上一双笨重的木屐，也就是那种木头做的鞋子。

卡尔的同学丝毫不顾忌他闷闷不乐的神色，拿他寒碜的衣着开了很多玩笑。卡尔尽量不把他们放在心上，也不理会他们说的话。过了一会儿，男孩们排好队，跟着老师，向教堂出发了。

在途中，男孩们开始说起家里为他们准备的美味晚餐。一个男孩告诉大家，他们家今晚准备了一只硕大的鹅。

另一个说，他会得到一只木箱子，里面是一棵小杉树，枝叶上挂满了橙子、糖果、玩具这些玩意。

男孩们还在猜测圣婴会送自己什么礼物。他会放什么礼物在他们的鞋子里呢？当然了，他们一定会记得把鞋子放在烟囱里，再上床睡觉。

小卡尔心里很清楚，他的阿姨是不会给他准备晚餐的，只会让他空着肚子上床。不过，他也会充满期待地把他的木屐放在壁炉里的灰堆上。他希望圣婴不会把他忘了，因为过去的每一年，他都在很努力地做一个又乖又勤快的孩子。

做完了礼拜，男孩子们跟着老师，两个两个地离开教堂。在教堂的门廊里，有个孩子坐在石凳上，睡得正香。天那么冷，他就只穿着亚麻袍子，光着两只脚丫。

他看上去不像是乞丐，因为他身上的袍子还是崭新崭新的。在他旁边的地上，还堆着一些木工的工具。

在星光的照耀下，这孩子的脸庞看起来是那么的甜美，金色的头发看起来像王冠一样闪闪发亮。只是，在十二月寒冷的夜晚之中，这孩子的脚却冻得发紫，让人不忍心直视。

穿着厚厚冬装的男孩们走过，都没有把那个陌生的小孩放在心上。卡尔是最后一个从教堂出来的，只有他停了下来，觉得这个睡着的孩子非常可怜。

"唉！"无父无母的卡尔对自己叹了口气，"这么冷的天，这个小孩还不得不光着脚走路，真是太可怜了。更糟的是，在他睡觉的时候，圣婴甚至不能在他鞋子里放点东西安慰他，因为他连可以装东西的木屐都没有。"

小卡尔把自己右脚的木屐脱下来，放在了熟睡的孩子身前。他跟着前面的男孩们，右脚松垮地套着袜子，一跛一跛地走在积雪里，回到了阿姨的家。

"瞧瞧这没用的家伙！"他的阿姨叫道。看到卡尔回来，右脚的鞋子却没了，她生气极了："你把木屐弄哪儿去了？"

当他把自己做的事告诉阿姨之后，她大声地嘲笑起他来。

"所以你是把你的鞋子给乞丐了？"她说道，"真新鲜！好，好，既然这样，我就把你另一只鞋放到烟囱里。我向你保证，今晚圣婴一定会在那儿留下点东西，好让我明天早上拿来抽你。"

"明天你只能吃干面包和水。"她继续说，"看看下次再来一个乞丐，你还敢不敢把你的鞋子给他。"

阿姨给了可怜的卡尔一点教训，然后把他赶回阁楼的床上睡觉。卡尔心里难过极了，他摸黑爬上了床，很快就睡着了。只是，他的泪水打湿了枕头。

第二天早上，老阿姨从楼上走下来。天哪！她看见了一幅十分美妙的景象！大烟囱里堆满了漂亮的玩具，成包成包上好的蜡烛，还有其他一切好东西！

昨天深夜里，她把那只左脚的鞋子放在这里，打算放根桦条进去，用它来惩罚卡尔，现在鞋子前却堆满了这些豪华的礼物。在旁边，还放着一只右脚的鞋子，正是昨天她外甥送给流浪儿的那一只。

两只鞋子都堆满了礼物。

小卡尔从楼上跑下来，站在这些漂亮的礼物前。这时，门外突然传来响亮的欢笑声。老阿姨和小卡尔走出门外，想看看发生了什么事。他们发现，邻居们都聚集在广场的喷泉周围。

到底发生了什么事呢？原来，之前那些光会期待漂亮礼物的孩子，什么都没得到。在他们的鞋子里，只有用来打人的棍子。哎，这真是又奇怪又好笑。

小孤儿卡尔和他的老阿姨想起了家里烟囱堆着的漂亮礼物，感到惊喜极了。

过了一会儿，他们看到牧师朝自己走过来，脸上还带着惊奇的神色。于是，人们突然明白了，那个以奇怪的姿态睡着，旁边还放着木工工具的漂亮孩子，其实就是圣婴啊。

（弗朗索瓦·戈贝）

♢ 作者介绍

弗朗索瓦·戈贝是法国诗人、小说家，他定居在巴黎。他的小说题材广泛，他最好的作品当中，有很多是为儿童创作的。1868年，弗朗索瓦·戈贝获得了法国荣誉军团勋章。

The Day Brothers

I have a story to tell you about seven brothers and their odd names. You see them all once every week. No two of them ever visit you at the same time, for as soon as one comes another goes.

They always come in the same order, and they all stay just the same length of time.

You never hear them, for they come and go without any noise. Just as the clocks strike twelve at midnight, one goes out and another comes in.

The names of the brothers sound very strange, but you will not wonder at that when I tell you that they are more than a thousand years old. Our great-great-grand-fathers named the brothers.

The first of the seven is called Sunday, and was named after the sun, just as you are named James, perhaps after your Uncle James; or your sister is named Annie, after your mamma.

The next was named Moon-day, after the moon; but we do not call it exactly by that name now. We say Monday, which means Moon-day.

The third was called Tiwes-day. Long ago people believed that strange beings lived in the clouds, or in the air, or among the stars, and that they would come to the earth, to help those who were in trouble.

The people of those days thought that these strange beings kept them from harm in battle, or helped them in hunting or farming. They called them gods, and believed them to be very much wiser and stronger than men.

It was thought that Tiw helped soldiers in battle and gave them victory over their enemies. So one of the brothers was named Tiwes-day, as I told you. We write it Tuesday now, but our great-great-grandfathers spelled it Tiwes-day.

Another brother was called Wodin's-day, after Wodin, who was said to be the wisest of all the gods. When we say Wednesday, it means Wodin's-day.

Wodin had a son called Thor, and the people named the fifth brother after him, Thor's-day; or as we say now, Thursday.

Wodin's wife was named Frig-ga, and it was from her that the next brother was named. Our grandfathers said Frig-ga's-day, but we say Friday, which is shorter and easier to say.

The last brother was called Saturn's-day. Saturn was another of the gods that people worshiped long ago. They thought that he once came and lived on the earth. He chose the beautiful land of Italy for his home.

The people were kind to him. In return, he taught them how to cultivate the land, and raise grain and grapes and figs and apples.

No wonder that people named one of the days after him. We say Saturday now, but long ago everybody said Saturn's-day.

译文

星期的故事

我要给你们讲一个故事，故事讲的是七个兄弟，还有他们的名字是怎么来的。你一周能见到每个兄弟一次，从来不会有两个兄弟同时拜访你，因为一个来了的话，另一个会马上走掉。

他们每次都以同样顺序来探望你，每次停留的时间也都一致。

你从未听过他们的声音，因为他们来来去去，悄无声息。就像时钟在十二点响起，一个刚离开，另一个就立刻赶到。

七兄弟的名字都特别奇怪，但只要我告诉你他们已经一千多岁了，你就丝毫不会觉得诧异了。他们的名字是我们的祖先取的。

七兄弟的老大叫太阳神日，是以太阳的名字命名的，就像你叫詹姆斯，是以詹姆斯叔叔名字命名，或者你的姐妹叫安妮，是以妈妈的名字命名一样。

接下来的兄弟叫月亮神日，是以月亮的名字命名的，但是我们现在基本上不用这个名字。我们叫他星期一，意思就是月亮日。

老三叫作战神日。很久以前，在云朵后面，在天空中，在星星上面，有一些陌生的生灵，他们会来到地球，帮助陷入困境中的人们。

那时的人们相信这些陌生的生灵会帮他们远离战争的伤害，或者会在他们耕种或者狩猎的时候给他们帮助。他们把这些生物称为神，他们相信，神远比人类聪明和强壮。

他们相信，打仗的时候，战神提尔能帮助士兵打败敌人。所以我告诉你，一星期中有一天命名为战神日，现在我们写作星期二，但是我们的祖先把这一天叫作战神日。

另一个兄弟叫作主神日，以奥丁的名字命名。据说，奥丁是诸神中最聪明的一位。当我们说星期三的时候，就是指主神日。

奥丁有一个儿子叫索尔，七兄弟中的老五就是用他的名字命名的，叫雷神日，或者，像我们现在所说的星期四。

奥丁的妻子叫弗丽嘉，七兄弟中的下一位就是以她的名字命名的，我们的祖先称之为夜神日，但我们现在称之为星期五，更短也更好说一些。

七兄弟中的最后一位叫作农神日。萨图努是人们信奉的另外一位神灵，人们相信他曾经来过地球，当时他住在美丽的意大利。

人类对他很友善，作为回报，他教人们如何耕种土地，培育粮食、葡萄、无花果，还有苹果等。

怪不得人们会拿他的名字命名这一天。我们现在把这一天叫作星期六，但是很久以前人们把这一天叫作农神日。

The Pony Engine

The thing that the little Pony Engine wanted to be the most in the world was the locomotive of the Pacific Express.

Once he raced it a little piece, and beat it, before the Express locomotive was under way. Indeed, he almost got in front of it on a switch. My, but his mother was scared! She just screamed to him with her whistle.

But the little Pony Engine didn't care.

He had beaten the Pacific Express in a hundred yards, and what was to hinder him from beating it as long as he chose?

So one dark, snowy, blustery afternoon, when his mother was off pushing some empty coal cars beyond Charlestown, the little Pony Engine got on the track in front of the Express. When he heard the conductor say "All aboard!" and saw the brakeman lean out and wave to the engineer, he darted off like lightning.

The Pony Engine was so excited for a while that he couldn't tell whether the Express was gaining on him or not; but after twenty or thirty miles, he thought that he heard it pretty near. Of course the Express locomotive was drawing a heavy train of cars, and had to make a stop now and then, so the Pony Engine did really gain a little. When he began to be scared he gained a great deal.

The first place where he began to feel sorry, and to want his mother, was in Hoosac Tunnel. He kept thinking, "What if the Pacific Express was to run over him there in the dark, and his mother away off there in Boston, looking for him among the side-tracks?"

He gave a shriek, and just then shot out of the tunnel. A number of locomotives were standing there at North Adams. One of them shouted to him as he flew by, "What's your hurry, little one?" And he just screamed back, "Pacific Express!" and never stopped to explain.

All through the long, dark night, whenever a locomotive hailed the Pony Engine, he just screamed, "Pacific Express!" and kept on. And the Express kept gaining. On, on he whizzed across New York State and Ohio and Indiana until he got to Chicago. And the Express kept gaining.

By that time he was so hoarse that he could hardly whisper, but he kept saying, "Pacific Express! Pacific Express!" and kept right on until he reached the Mississippi River.

There he found a long train of freight cars on the bridge. He couldn't wait, and so he slipped down from the track to the edge of the river and jumped across. Then he scrambled up the bank to the track again.

After that he had a little rest, for the Express had to wait for the freight train to get off the bridge. So the Pony Engine stopped at the first station for a drink of water and a mouthful of coal, and then he flew ahead again.

At Omaha a kind old locomotive tried to find out where the Pony Engine belonged, and what his mother's name was, but the little thing was so bewildered that he could not tell. And the Express kept gaining.

On the plains he was chased by a pack of prairie wolves, but he left them behind. The antelopes were scared half to death.

He thought now that if he could only beat the Express to the Sierras, he could keep the start the rest of the way. He could get over the mountain more quickly than the Express, and might be in San Francisco before the Express got to Sacramento.

The Express kept gaining. But the Pony Engine just zipped along the upper edge of Kansas and the lower edge of Nebraska, and on through Colorado and Utah and Nevada. When he got to the Sierras, he stopped a little, and went over them like a goat. He just doubled up his fore wheels under him, and jumped.

By this time the Pony Engine couldn't say "Pacific Express" any more, and he didn't try. He just said. "Express! Express!" and then "Press! Press!"and then "Ess! Ess!" and pretty soon only "Ss! Ss!"

Before they reached San Francisco, the Express locomotive's cowcatcher was almost touching the Pony Engine. He gave one howl of anguish as he felt the hot breath of the locomotive. Then he tore through the end of the San Francisco depot, and plunged into the Pacific Ocean.

(William Dean Howells)

译文

小火车头的故事

小火车头在这个世界上最想干的一件事就是打败太平洋特快列车的机车头。

有一次,在快车机车头启程之前,他和它比试了一下,并且打败了它。事实上,他几乎从一开始就是领先的。但他妈妈却非常担心,她鸣响汽笛,冲他尖声呼啸起来。

但是小火车头并不在意。

他已经超过了太平洋特快列车一百码,还有什么能阻挡他把它甩得更远呢?

于是,在一个北风呼啸、大雪纷飞的阴沉下午,小火车头占据了快车前面的轨道。他的妈妈不在,她要把一些空的运煤车厢推过查尔斯镇。小火车头听见售票员说"所有人上车",还看见司闸员探出身向司机挥手。就在此刻,他像闪电一样冲了出去。

有一会儿,小火车头兴奋过了头,都不知道快车是不是正在赶上来。但是四五十千米过后,他觉得他听见了它在靠近的声音。显然,由于快车头拖着一列装满小汽车的沉重车厢,并且还得不时地停一下,小火车头确实要领先那么一点儿。当他开始感到害怕的时候,他已经领先很多了。

在湖沙克隧道,他第一次感到难过,并且想要妈妈。他止不住地想着,如果太平洋特快列车在黑暗里超过了他怎么办?如果他远在波士顿的妈妈在旁轨间寻找他怎么办?

他发出一声尖叫,随之冲出了隧道。很多机车头正站在北亚当斯,当他飞掠而过的时候,其中一个机车头冲他喊道:"小东西,你急什么呢?"小火车头没有停下来解释,只是尖声回道:"太平洋特快列车!"

在漫长的黑夜里,每当有机车头向小火车头打招呼的时候,他总是一边尖叫着"太平洋特快列车",一边毫不停歇地向前跑。但是快车总是比他更快。他飕飕地掠过纽约州、俄亥俄州和印第安纳州,直到芝加哥。快车仍然在继续追赶。

到后来,小火车头嘶哑得几乎说不出话来,但他仍然不停地说着"太平洋特快列车!太平洋特快列车",在他到达密西西比河之前,他一直这样做。

那里的桥上停着一列长长的货车。他等不及,于是从铁轨上滑到了河边,然后跳了过去。接着他爬上岸,重新回到了轨道上。

之后他休息了一会,因为太平洋特快列车必须得等到货车离开大桥后才能通行。所以小火车头停在了第一个站台,喝了一口水,吃上一口煤,再次跑在了前头。

在奥马哈市,一个和蔼的老机车头想弄明白小火车头从哪里来,他妈妈是谁。但是这个小东西非常茫然,什么都说不出来。快车仍在继续追赶。

在平原上小火车头被一群草原狼追赶,但他把它们抛在了后面。羚羊们则被吓得半死。

现在他在考虑,也许只有到了内华达州的雪山才能打败快车,因为他比快车爬山更快,然后他就可以在剩余的路途上保持优势,可能当快车到达萨克拉门托的时候,他已经在圣佛朗西斯科了。

快车还在后面追赶。但是小火车头只是在堪萨斯州和内布拉斯加州之间的边界上蜿蜒前进,并且穿过了科罗拉多州、犹他州和内华达州。当他到达雪山的时候,他停了一会儿,然后像山羊一样攀越了过去。他把前面的轮子折到身体下面,然后跳起来。

这时候小火车头已经疲累得再也说不出"太平洋特快列车"了,他也放弃了尝试,只是说着"特快列车!特快列车",然后变成"特快车!特快车",再变成"快车!快车",最后只剩下"快!快"了。

在他们到达圣佛朗西斯科之前,快车机车头的排障器几乎碰到了小火车头。当他感受到机车头喷出的热气时,随即发出了一声痛苦的哀号,飞快地撞出了圣佛朗西斯科站台,一头扎进了太平洋。

(威廉姆·迪恩·豪厄尔斯)

✍ 作者介绍

威廉姆·迪恩·豪厄尔斯早年生活在俄亥俄州。他将这些经历以一种迷人的方式写进了《一个男孩的城镇》和《波尼·贝克的飞行》中。

豪厄尔斯先生创作了许多小说、游记,还写过一些诗歌。他是专业的儿童文学作家。其《每天都是圣诞节》一书中收录了故事《每天都是圣诞节》《南瓜戈洛瑞》以及本文。该书由哈柏兄弟出版社出版。

练习

1.抄写
Little, spelling, remember
Children, crimson, locomotive

_____

_____

The Swiss Clock's Story

"Cuckoo! Cuckoo!" said a busy little gentleman, popping his head out of an open door. "It's time somebody asked me to tell all that I know. Pray, what is the use of my stepping up every half-hour to remind you that I am here, if I am never to have a chance to speak?"

"I'm ready, if you are, Mr. Cuckoo," answered Robert, laughing at his fussy little ways.

"In a valley, in view of a lake fed by the noisy waters of a glacier stream, I first saw the light," said the Cuckoo. He now lived in a carved Swiss clock, hanging upon the wall of the Standish drawing-room.

"The house that my maker lived in was one of a village of little wooden houses with overhanging roofs kept in place by large stones. This was to provide against the fierce gusts of wind that swept the street in winter, and threatened to lift the roofs.

"The houses were built so closely together that one could almost shake hands with their neighbors across the street by leaning from the window. Most of the houses had curved balconies around them.

"Up under the eaves of the roofs hung corn, put there to dry for the cows, horses, goats, and poultry, which lived on the ground floor during the cold season. The animals were separated from the family above only by a flooring of thin planks.

"The cart was kept in the yard leaning against the house-wall. When the horse was to be harnessed to it, he had only to step out of one of the doorways of the dwelling. Nothing could be more convenient, when the great snows fell.

"In this village there were several wood-carvers of whom my maker was the chief. Sometimes they would band together to work and chat.

"There it was that I heard many interesting tales about the race of dwarfs, or Hill-men, who once lived in the clefts and caverns of the surrounding mountains.

"The Hill-men were said to be friendly enough to deserving people, but they did not mind flying into a terrible rage, if their wills were crossed.

"In winter, when the outer world was one vast field of ice and snow and frowning granite; when only the great glacier, dividing the highest mountains, lit at morning and at evening with a rosy glow from the snow; when howling winds bent the fir-trees low upon the cliffs——then the Hill-men were never seen abroad.

"A merry fellow and full of roguish tricks, was the Swiss Hill-man, in spite of his hot temper. He was kind, and generous, too.

"If a weak child was sent by its parents to fetch home firewood, often would they find a neatly made bundle of sticks lying across the forest-path.

"Sometimes a poor old crone would discover in her hay-shed a dozen pearly eggs where she had hoped for but one; and sometimes, at the elbow of the toiling woodsman, a bowl of frothing milk would appear.

"Many a stray lamb he drove back to the fold, and many a shepherd he guided to where his missing herds were grazing.

"One of the pleasant stories about the valley-roaming dwarfs was as follows: One day an honest laborer named Bartel went out with his little son to plow a field, which he meant to sow with grain.

"Bartel was not a skilled hand with his plow, and he felt very anxious about the success of his work, since, lately, all his sheep had died, and poverty was staring him in the face.

"From dawn till noon, the father and son worked patiently, turning the grassy soil in furrows, the sweat rolling from their foreheads.

"The boy, who was very tired, stopped to rest. Looking over at the rocky heights beyond, he saw smoke rising from a hill-top, while the air was filled with the smell of savory cooking.

"'Look, father!' cried the lad. 'There is the smoke from the Hill-men's kitchen. No doubt they are making ready for a feast. How good their cooking smells when one has had nothing to eat but a crust of bread since morning! Ah, if we had but one little dish——whether roast boiled, or baked I care not——out of their plenty!'

"The father sighed, for he had nothing to give his child. Silently he plowed on, when lo! A wonder appeared. There, right in the middle of a furrow, upon a napkin of fine white linen, lay a silver dish, heaped with roast beef, and beside it a loaf of bread.

"'Hurrah! Long live the generous dwarfs!' cried father and son together. They ate plentifully of the good meal, and were careful to put the silver platter, fork, and napkin back where they had been found.

"By the time that they had made the round of the field again, every one of the belongings of the dwarfs had vanished, excepting the damask cloth. This Bartel took home as a token of luck to come, and for many, many years the curious little cloth was handed down in his family.

"From the day of their unexpected feast, Bartel and his son prospered in all that they tried to do, and in time came to be the rich folk of the neighborhood."

(Mrs. Burton Harrison, adapted)

译文

瑞士钟的故事

"布谷！布谷！"一扇打开的门里，一位忙碌的小绅士伸出头来，叫道："有人叫我把知道的事情都说出来，现在是时候了。每隔半小时，我都走出来提醒你，我还在这里。请问，我要是永远没有机会说话，那这样的提醒又有什么用呢？"

"布谷先生，只要你愿意讲，我就愿意听。"罗伯特露出了他略带挑剔的笑容。

"在一个山谷里，'哗哗'作响的冰川水形成了湖泊，我也因此第一次见到了光。"布谷先生说。斯坦迪什的客厅挂着一个在墙上'梆梆'作响的瑞士雕刻钟，他如今就住这里面。

"制造我的人住在一个村庄的小木屋里。屋顶和屋檐靠大石块来固定，冬天时，狂风呼啸着卷过街道，这样的结构才能起到抵挡的作用。

"那里的房子大多都围有曲形的阳台，挨挤地建在一起。人们只要从窗户伸出手,几乎都能穿过街道和邻居握手了。

"屋檐上挂着玉米,风干之后,就是牛、马、羊和家禽冬天的口粮。在那时,畜生们就住在人的楼下,中间只隔着一层薄薄的木地板。

"运货车靠着宅子的墙,停在院子里。主人只需走过宅子的其中一个门廊,就能给车套上马匹。下大雪时,做什么都还是很方便。

"村子里有好几个做雕刻的木工师父,制造我的匠人就是其中的头头。有时,他们会聚在一起工作、闲聊。

"我也因此听到了许多有趣的故事,都是关于矮人族的。他们又叫山洞人,曾经住在附近的山谷和洞穴里。

"听说,山洞人对友善的人很友善。但是,一旦把他们惹火了,他们就会大发脾气。

"冬天,外面的世界只能看见一片辽阔的冰雪,还有凸出的花岗岩。只有宽大的冰川在海拔最高的山脉间淌过,在清晨和傍晚都反射出玫瑰色的光芒。狂风咆哮着,吹弯了悬崖上杉木的腰。这时,就不会在外面看到山洞人的踪迹了。

"瑞士山洞人里有一个开心的家伙,他既慷慨又善良,脑子里满是恶作剧的把戏。不过,他的脾气也很火爆。

"要是有哪个父母使唤一个弱不禁风的孩子,要他拾烧火的木柴回家。那他多半会发现,森林的小道间就横放着一捆整整齐齐的木柴。

"要是有个穷苦的老妇人希望得到一只鸡蛋,她有时就会发现,在自家的草堆上就放着一打珍贵的鸡蛋。有时,干着苦工的樵夫手边,也会出现一碗泡沫丰盈的牛奶。

"他会把许多迷路的羔羊赶回羊圈。很多牧羊人弄丢了羊群,他也会把他们指引到羊群正在吃草的地方。

"小矮人在山谷间流连,发生了许多美好的故事。其中一个是这样的。有一个诚实的劳动者,他的名字叫巴特尔。有一天,他准备播种点谷子,就带着小儿子去犁一块田。

"最近,他养的羊全部死了。巴特尔十分忧虑,因为他不太会犁地,所以怕连犁地也失败了,这样他很快就会沦为一个穷人了。

"从黎明到黑夜,父子俩耐心地工作着,把长满草的泥土翻到犁沟里,汗珠不断地从他们额头上滚落下来。

"儿子累了，就停下来休息。他的目光越过了岩石，看见一个小山头里升起了炊烟，空气中弥漫着食物的诱人香气。

"'爸爸快看！'他叫道，'山洞人的厨房里有烟冒出来了，不用说，他们一定在准备一顿大餐。我们从早上到现在，就吃了点面包皮，对于我们来说，他们煮的东西味道真是太香了！啊！这样丰盛的大餐，我不在乎是煮的还是烤的——如果我们能尝上一点儿——'

"父亲并没有东西可以给孩子吃，叹了叹气，沉默地犁着地。直到——看！神奇的事情发生了。在犁沟中间，铺有一张上好的白色亚麻餐巾，上面还放着一个银色盘子，里面堆着烤好的牛肉，旁边还放着一条面包。

"'太棒了！慷慨的小矮人万岁！'父子俩一起欢呼起来。他们美餐一顿，并小心翼翼地把银盘、叉子和餐巾放回了原位。

"当他们再次回到田里时，小矮人的东西都消失了，只剩下那块带着花纹的餐巾。巴特尔把它带了回家，以纪念这次的好运。这么多年以来，这一小块神奇的布一直在他家族里传承了下来。

"吃了这顿天降的大餐以后，巴特尔和儿子不论做什么事，都能取得成功。不久，他们就成为了乡邻之中的富人了。"

（伯顿·哈里森女士）

✎ 作者介绍

哈里斯女士出生于弗吉尼亚州，她一生都在那里度过。她曾到欧洲学习，也去过那儿旅游，她还在亚洲、非洲旅行过。哈里斯女士大多数作品都是写给成年人看的，但她写给孩子们的作品《过去的童话故事书》《民间和童话故事》以及《小摆设的故事》都是优秀的作品。《瑞士钟的故事》正是选自后一本书，由查尔斯·斯克里布纳家族出版公司出版。

The New Year Came of Age

The Old Year being dead, the New Year came of age, which he does, by Calendar Law, as soon as the breath is out of the old gentleman's body. Nothing would serve the youth but that he must give a dinner upon the occasion, to which all the Days of the year were invited.

The Festivals, whom he appointed as his stewards, were mightily taken with the notion. They had been engaged time out of mind, they said, in providing mirth and cheer for mortals below; and it was time that they should have a taste of their bounty.

All the Days came to the dinner. Covers were provided for three hundred and sixty-five guests at the principal table; with an occasional knife and fork at the sideboard for the Twenty-Ninth of February.

I should have told you that cards of invitation had been sent out. The carriers were the Hours; twelve as merry little whirligig foot-pages as you should desire to see. They went all round, and found out the persons invited well enough, with the exception of Easter Day, Shrove Tuesday, and a few such Movables, who had lately shifted their quarters.

Well, they were all met at last, four Days, five Days, all sorts of Days, and a rare din they made of it. There was nothing but "Hail fellow Day I well met, brother Day, sister Day"——only Lady Day kept a little on the aloof and seemed somewhat scornful. Yet some said, Twelfth Day cut her out, for she came in a silk suit, white and gold, like a queen on a frost-cake, all royal and glittering.

The rest came, some in green, some in white——but Lent and his family were not yet out of mourning. Rainy Days came in dripping, and sunshiny Days helped them to change their stockings. Wedding Day was there in his marriage finery. Pay Day came late, as he always does; and Doomsday sent word——he might be expected.

April Fool (as my young lord's jester) took upon himself to marshal the guests. And wild work he made of it; good Days, bad Days, all were shuffled together. He had stuck the Twenty-First of June next to the

Twenty-Second of December, and the former looked like a May-pole beside a marrow-bone. Ash Wednesday got wedged in between Christmas and Lord Mayor's Day.

At another part of the table, Shrove Tuesday was helping the Second of September to some broth, which courtesy the latter returned with the delicate thigh of a pheasant. The Last of Lent was springing upon Shrovetide's pancakes; April Fool, seeing this, told him that he did well, for pancakes were proper to a good Friday.

When it began to grow a little duskish, Candlemas lustily called for lights, but this was opposed by all the Days, who protested against burning daylight.

May Day, with that sweetness which is her own, made a neat speech proposing the health of the founder. This being done, the lordly New Year from the upper end of the table, in a cordial but somewhat lofty tone, returned thanks.

They next fell to quibbles and conundrums. The question being proposed, who had the greatest number of followers——the Quarter Days said there could be no question as to that; for they had all the creditors in the world dogging their heels. But April Fool gave it in favor of the Forty Days before Easter; because the debtors in all cases outnumbered the creditors, and they kept Lent all the year.

All this while Valentine's Day kept courting pretty May, who sat next him, slipping love-letters under the table, till the Dog Days (who are naturally of warm temper) began to be jealous, and to bark and rage.

April Fool, who likes a bit of sport above measure, clapped and hallooed them on; and as fast as their anger cooled, those mad wags, the Ember Days, were at it with their bellows, to blow it into a flame.

At last, day being ended, the Days called for their cloaks and greatcoats, and took their leaves. Lord Mayor's Day went off in a Mist as usual; Shortest Day in a deep black Fog, which wrapped the little gentleman all round like a hedgehog.

Two Vigils, or watchmen, saw Christmas Day safe home. Another Vigil——a stout, sturdy patrol, called the Eve of St. Christopher——

escorted Ash Wednesday.

Longest Day set off westward in beautiful crimson and gold——the rest, some in one fashion, some in another; but **Valentine** and pretty **May** took their departure together in one of the prettiest silvery twilight that a **Lover's Day** could wish to set in.

(Charles Lamb)

译文

新年的成人礼

旧年正在慢慢死去，等到这位老绅士呼出他的最后一口气，根据日历法，新年也就正式成人了。这位年轻人得不到什么招待，但他必须准备晚宴，邀请一年中的所有日子前来。

那些被他任命为管理员的节假日们很喜欢这个主意。很久以来，他们就一直忙碌着，给下面的凡人们带来欢声笑语。现在，轮到他们来品尝他们曾给予别人的慷慨馈赠了。

所有的日子都奔赴晚宴。桌子上已经摆好了365个客人的餐具；此外，还有给2月29日准备的特殊的刀叉。

我应该告诉过你，邀请函早已寄出。快递员就是小时们；你应该很乐意见到的，那十二个年轻的侍者，个个欢乐得像小陀螺似的。他们不远万里，找到那些已经受邀的日子。而像复活节、忏悔日这样变动的节日，最近还在换班，所以不太容易找到。

好了，他们终于都见面了。四个，五个，各种各样的日子，真是难得的热闹。极其要好的朋友们碰面了，兄弟姐妹们也都碰面了。只是那些女士们有点冷漠，看起来还有几分轻蔑。不过有人说，主显节不搭理人，是因为她穿了一身丝绸套装，纯白与金色搭配，像冻蛋糕上的女王一样，有一种皇家的气质。

剩下的日子们也来了，有穿绿色的，有穿白色的——但大斋节和他的家人们还很哀伤。雨天们进来时还滴着水，晴天们就去帮他们换双长袜。婚庆日穿着一身婚礼的华服。发薪日来晚了，他总是这样；世界末日发来消息——他可能会来。

愚人节（他是我的小主人的御用小丑）主动承担起安排客人就座的任务，然而他总是胡来；好日子和坏日子，都被排到一块儿去了。他把6月21日和11月22日排到了一起，这看起来像五朔节花桩和一根髓骨并排放在一起一样奇怪。他还让圣灰节挤在圣诞节和伦敦市长就职日之间。

桌子的另一边，忏悔节正在帮9月2日盛些肉汤，而后者有礼貌地回赠了他一块清淡可口的鸡腿肉。大斋节的最后一天扑向了忏悔节的薄煎饼；愚人节看到之后，称赞他干得好，因为薄煎饼和"油炸节"很般配。

当灯光逐渐暗淡下来的时候，圣烛节强烈要求要把光打亮，但所有不允许白日点灯的日子都反对这个提议。

劳动节，以她独有的可爱态度，发表了简短的讲话，并提议所有人一起祝宴会的主人一切安康。祝词结束后，气质高贵的新年先生，从酒桌的上等座、以热忱但略显高傲的语气向他们致谢。

之后大家就围绕着一个难题争辩开了。支持季度结算日的人最多，因为世界上所有的债主都得听他的。但是比起复活节，愚人节更支持大斋节；因为大斋节让欠债的人比债主还多，他们总是在过大斋"借"。

这会儿，情人节正在追求坐在他身边的五月美人儿，从桌子底下给她传情书。三伏天们（他们天生是个暴脾气）吃醋了，愤怒地叫了起来，搅黄了这件事。

愚人节，喜欢玩点出格的，他鼓起掌来，还朝他们大喊大叫，瞎起哄；四季节的热情和他们的怒火冷却的一样快，这会儿他们的劲头也上来了，都在煽风点火。

最终，一天要结束了。日子们都拿起自己的斗篷和外衣，纷纷告辞。伦敦市长就职日和往常一样在雾气中离开了；日长最短的一天身披黑色的浓雾，裹得活像个刺猬。

两个值夜的护卫，或者叫守护者，负责护送圣诞节安全到家。另一个值夜护卫——一个矮胖的结实的巡逻员，圣·克里斯托弗前夕——负责护送圣灰节。

日长最长的一天，穿着金色与深红相间的外衣，向西出发——剩下的节日都各自离开了；只有情人节和漂亮的五月，在银白色暮光中，相依离去。

（查尔斯·兰姆）

The Three Wishes

Once upon a time, and be sure it was a long time ago, there lived a poor woodman in a great forest. Every day of his life he went out to cut timber.

One day, as he started out, the good wife filled his wallet and slung his bottle on his back, that he might have meat and drink in the forest. He had marked out for his work this day a huge old oak, which, he thought, would furnish many and many a good plank.

When he came to the oak, he took his ax in his hands and swung it round his head as though he had a mind to fell the tree at one stroke. But he had not given one blow, when there stood before him a fairy, who prayed him to spare the tree.

The woodman was dazed, as you may fancy, with wonder and fright, and he could not open his mouth to utter a word. He found his tongue at last. "Well," said he, "I'll even do as you wish."

"You have done better for yourself than you know," said the fairy. "To show that I am grateful, I will grant your next three wishes, let them be what they may."

With that the fairy was no more to be seen, so the woodman slung his wallet over his shoulder and his bottle at his side, and off he started for home.

But the way was long, and the poor man was still dazed with the wonderful thing that had happened to him. When he got home there was nothing in his mind but the wish to sit down and rest.

Maybe, too, it was a trick of the fairy's. Who can tell? Anyhow, down he sat by the blazing fire; and as he sat, he became hungry, though it was a long way from supper-time.

"Hast thou naught for supper, dame?" said he to his wife.

"Nay, not for two hours," said she.

"Ah!" groaned the woodman, "I wish i had a good link of black pudding here before me."

No sooner had he said the word, than clatter, clatter, rustle, rustle, what should come down the chimney but a link of the finest black pudding the heart of man could wish for?

If the woodman stared, the good wife stared three times as much. "What's all this?" said she.

Then all the morning's work came back to the wood-man, and he told his tale right out, from beginning to end. As he told it, the good wife became angry.

When he had made an end of the story, she burst out, "Thou art but silly, Jan, thou art but silly! I wish the pudding were at thy nose, I do, indeed!"

And in a twinkling there sat the good man with his nose the longer for a noble link of black pudding.

He gave a pull, but it stuck, and she gave a pull, but it stuck; and they both pulled till they had nigh pulled the nose off, but the pudding stuck and stuck.

"What's to be done now?" said he.

"It does not look so very bad," said she, looking hard at him.

Then the woodman saw that if he wished, he must wish in a hurry, and so he wished that the black pudding might come off his nose.

Well!——There it lay in a dish on the table. So it happened that if the good man and good wife did not ride in a golden coach, or dress in silk and satin, they had at least as fine a black pudding for their supper as the heart of man could desire.

(Joseph Jacobs)

译文

三个愿望

很久很久以前，深林里住着一位可怜的伐木工，他每天都外出砍伐木材。有一天，在他临出门的时候，他的妻子给他的包里装满食物，帮他把水壶挎在背上，这样他就可以在森林里喝水吃饭了。他已经在一棵老橡树上做了标记，打算今天把它砍倒。他想，这肯定能做成很多很多的优质木板。

他来到了那颗大树边，拿出斧头，高高地举过头顶，好像一下子就能将这棵树给撂倒。但他还没来得及砍下去，一位仙女出现在他的眼前，求他放过这棵大树。

伐木工呆住了，你能想象得出，他又惊又怕，简直说不出话来。最后，他终于回过神来。"好吧，"他说道，"就按你说的做吧！"

"你无意之间帮了你自己一个大忙，"仙女说道，"为了表达我的感激，我会保证你接下来的三个愿望都能够成真。"

话音刚落，仙女就不见了身影，伐木工也把包挎在肩上，水杯挎在腰间，准备回家了。

在回家的漫漫长路中，伐木工仍然对刚刚发生的事情感到很茫然。他回到家中，脑中一片空白，只想着赶紧坐下休息一会。

也许，这就是仙女的一个恶作剧罢了，谁知道呢？不管怎样，他坐在了燃烧的壁炉旁，刚坐下，就感到腹中一阵饥饿，可是现在离晚饭时间还早得很呐。

"你有没有做晚饭呀？"他问妻子道。

"没，再等两个小时吧！"妻子说。

"哎，"伐木工发起了牢骚，"要是有一串上好的黑香肠在我面前就好了。"

话音刚落，噼里啪啦，一串黑香肠从烟囱里面滚了下来。这不就是伐木工想要的那种上好的黑香肠么？

如果说伐木工惊讶地睁大了眼睛，那么他妻子的眼睛就瞪得比他还大三倍。"这是怎么回事？"妻子问道。

这时，他想起来早上的离奇经历，于是便把故事原原本本、从头至尾都告诉了妻子。妻子越听越气。

他刚把故事说完，妻子便爆发了："你就是个蠢货，真的，你就是个蠢货！我真希望这串香肠能长在你的鼻子上！"

突然一阵亮光闪现，妻子面前的丈夫鼻子变长了许多，上面挂着一串上好的黑香肠！

他试图把这串香肠拽下来，可是没有成功。妻子也赶紧去帮忙，还是没有拽动。两个人一起去拽，似乎都要把鼻子拽下来了，可是香肠还是纹丝不动。

"我们现在怎么办呢？"他说道。

"你这看起来还不是很糟。"妻子说道，眼睛凝视着他。

伐木工想着，如果他要许愿，必须赶紧，于是他许愿，让这串黑香肠赶紧从自己的鼻子上下来吧。

好吧！——香肠最后落在了饭桌的碟子里。所以，尽管这对善良的夫妻没有能够坐上黄金马车，也没能够穿上高级绸缎。最起码，他们的晚餐有黑香肠吃了，那可是伐木工心里渴望的食物呢！

（约瑟夫·雅各布）

作者介绍

约瑟夫·雅各布生于澳大利亚，后居美国。他比本国任何一个人都熟悉神话故事，他的到来总会引起孩子们的热烈欢迎。他的著作中包含了《英国童话》《凯尔特童话》和《印度童话》。《三个愿望》取自于一本名为《英国童话续编》的书，由G.P. 普特南家族出版公司出版。

练习

把下列句子改成祈使句。

1. Sir Galahad to take a seat at the Round Table.
2. A friend to write you a letter.
3. Children how to act toward their parents.
4. A woodman not to cut down a tree.
5. Some one to close the door.

Chapter 6
Miscellaneous Poems | 杂诗

预习

anxious /ˈæŋkʃəs/ 担心的
astonishing /əˈstɑːnɪʃɪŋ/ 震惊的
exclaim /ɪkˈskleɪm/ 大声说
fault /fɔːlt/ 犯错
modestly /ˈmɒdɪstli/ 谨慎地
publisher /ˈpʌblɪʃər/ 出版商
recovered /rɪˈkʌvəd/ 康复
remarkable /rɪˈmɑːrkəbl/ 惊人的
senses /sens/ 感觉
stammer /ˈstæmər/ 结巴着说
suppose /səˈpoʊz/ 假定
thrust /θrʌst/ 插入

Hiawatha's Sailing

"Give me of your bark, O Birch Tree!
Of your yellow bark, O Birch Tree!
Growing by the rushing river,
Tall and stately in the valley!
I a light canoe will build me,
That shall float upon the river,
Like a yellow leaf in autumn,
Like a yellow water-lily!

"Lay aside your cloak, O Birch Tree!
Lay aside your white-skin wrapper,
For the summer-time is coming,
And the sun is warm in heaven,
And you need no white-skin wrapper!"

This aloud cried Hiawatha,
In the solitary forest,
When the birds were singing gaily,
In the Moon of Leaves were singing,
And the tree with all its branches,
Rustled in the breeze of morning,
Saying, with a sigh of patience,
"Take my cloak, O Hiawatha!"

With his knife the tree he girdled;
Just beneath its lowest branches,
Just above the roots, he cut it,
Till the sap came oozing outward,
Down the trunk, from top to bottom,
Sheer he cleft the bark asunder,
With a wooden wedge he raised it,
Stripped it from the trunk unbroken.

"Give me of your boughs, O Cedar!
Of your strong and pliant branches,
My canoe to make more steady,
Make more strong and firm beneath me!"
Through the summit of the Cedar,
Went a sound, a cry of horror,
Went a murmur of resistance;
But it whispered, bending downward,
"Take my boughs, O Hiawatha!"

Down he hewed the boughs of cedar,
Shaped them straightway to a framework,
Like two bows he formed and shaped them,
Like two bent bows together.

"Give me of your roots, O Tamarack!
Of your fibrous roots, O Larch Tree!
My canoe to bind together,
So to bind the ends together,
That the water may not enter,
That the river may not wet me!"

And the Larch, with all its fibers,
Shivered in the air of morning,
Touched his forehead with its tassels,
Said, with one long sigh of sorrow,
"Take them all, O Hiawatha!"
From the earth he tore the fibers,
Tore the tough roots of the Larch tree,
Closely sewed the bark together,
Bound it closely to the framework.

"Give me of your balm, O Fir Tree!
Of your balsam and your resin,
So to close the seams together
That the water may not enter,
That the river may not wet me!"

And the Fir Tree, tall and somber,
Sobbed through all its robes of darkness,
Rattled like a shore with pebbles,
Answered and weeping,
"Take my balm, O Hiawatha!"

And he took the tears of balsam,
Took the resin of the Fir Tree,
Seamed therewith each seam and fissure,
Made each crevice safe from water.

"Give me of your quills O Hedgehog!
I will make a necklace of them,
Make a girdle for my beauty,
And two stars to deck her bosom!"

From a hollow tree the Hedgehog
With his sleepy eyes looked at him,
Shot his shining quills, like arrows,
Saying, with a drowsy murmur,
Through the tangle of his whiskers
"Take my quills, O Hiawatha!"

From the ground the quills he gathered,
All the little shining arrows,
Stained them blue and red and yellow,
With the juice of roots and berries;
Into his canoe he wrought them,
Round its waist a shining girdle,
Round its bows a gleaming necklace,
On its breast two stars resplendent.

Thus the Birch Canoe was built,
In the valley, by the river,
In the bosom of the forest;

And the forest's life was in it,
All its mystery and its magic,
All the lightness of the birch tree,

All the toughness of the cedar,
All the larch's supple sinews;
And it floated on the river,
Like a yellow leaf in autumn,
Like a yellow water-lily.

(Henry Wadsworth Longfellow)

译文

海华沙的航行

"给我你的树皮,哦,桦树,
你那黄色的树皮。
你长在急流冲刷的河边,
高大雄伟地立在溪谷里!
我将造一只轻巧的独木舟,
它会漂浮在河面上,
像秋天里的一片黄叶,
像一朵黄色的水仙!

"丢掉你的保护,哦,桦树!
丢掉保护你的那白皮,
因为夏日正在来临,
天空里的太阳照得温暖,
你不需要这白皮!"

海华沙喊声响亮,
在他隐居的森林。
此时鸟儿们在快乐地歌唱,
在树冠里歌唱。

而桦树舞动所有的树枝，
在清晨的微风里沙沙作响，
容忍地叹了一口气，说：
"拿走我的树皮，哦，海华沙！"

他带着刀子绕树一圈；
在最低的树枝之下，
在树根之上，他割下去，
直到树液缓缓渗到外面，
沿着树干，从顶端到底部，
他完全割离树皮，
用一个木楔撬出，
将它完好无损地剥离了树干。

"给我你的树枝，哦，杉树！
你那强壮柔韧的树枝，
我的独木舟要造得更坚固，
让它在我身下更结实更稳固！"
从杉树的顶端，
响起一声恐惧的哭喊，
响起一声反抗的喃喃；
但它弯下身来轻声说：
"拿走我的树枝，哦，海华沙！"

他砍下杉树的大树枝，
立即把它们做成独木舟的框架，
他还做出两个船头的形状，
两个一起弯曲的船头形状。

"给我你的根须，哦，松树！
你那纤细的根须，哦，松树！

我的独木舟要捆绑在一起，
把船底绑在一起，
这样河水才不会进来，
这样河水才不会把我弄湿！"

松树抖着所有根须，
在清晨的空气里颤动，
用花穗触碰他的额头，
悲伤地长叹一声，说：
"拿走它们吧，哦，海华沙！"
他从土地里扯出根须，
扯出松树坚韧的根须，
将树皮严密地缝在一起，
把它紧紧绑在框架上。

"给我你的香油，哦，枞树！
你的香膏，你的树脂，
让我填满那些缝隙，
这样河水才不会进来，
这样河水才不会把我弄湿！"

枞树高高站着，忧郁无比，
呜咽响起在它所有黑暗的阴影里，
就好像布满卵石的河岸，
流着泪痛哭着回答：
"拿走我的香油，哦，海华沙！"

他拿走了泪滴般的香膏，
拿走了枞树的树脂，
填满了每一条裂口和缝隙，
让每一个缺口都远离水的侵袭。

"给我你的刺,哦,箭猪!
我将用它们做一条项链,
为我的美人做一条项链,
再把两颗星星装饰在她的胸前!"

从一棵空心树里钻出了箭猪,
用睡意蒙眬的双眼看着他,
它那闪亮的刺像箭一样向他射去,
它在纠缠的细须里,
昏昏欲睡地咕哝着:
"拿走我的刺,哦,海华沙!"

他收集地上的刺,
那所有光芒闪烁的小小之箭,
用树根和浆果的汁液;
把它们染成蓝的红的黄的,
他把它们装饰进独木舟,
它的腰部环绕着一条闪亮的腰带,
它的船头环绕着一条耀眼的项链,
它的胸前点缀着两颗光彩夺目的星子。

桦树独木舟就这样造好了,
在溪谷里,在小河边,
在森林的胸膛深处;

它拥有森林的生命,
和它所有的神秘和魔力,
它有桦树的轻巧,
杉树的坚强,
松树柔韧的力量;
它漂浮在河面上,

像秋天里的一片黄叶，
像一朵黄色的水仙！

（亨利·沃兹沃思·朗费罗）

练习

1. 抄写

（1）And the forest's life was in it.

_____

2. 仿照下列形式变形。

And the forest's life was in it. → And the life of the forest was in it.

（1）Through thy torn brim's jaunty grace. →

_____

（2）Health that mocks at doctor's rules. → _____

（3）Of the wild bee's morning chase. → _____

（4）Of the wild flower's time and place. → _____

A Close Race

The sun was bright, the sky was blue,
It was so fair a day,
The wind sprang up, drew in his breath,
And said, "Come out and play!"
The little waves cried, "Wait for us,
Before the sport begins!"
Then they tied their little white caps fast,
Beneath their dimpled chins.

"Now," cried the wind, "we'll have a race,
And see who first can reach,
By running fast and running far,
The line of yellow beach!"
The little waves ran hand in hand,
To win was all their mind;
With steady step and eager breath,
The wind ran close behind.

"Oh!" cried the waves, "the race is ours!
We're first to reach the land!"
"Ho!" laughed the wind, then pushed them all,
Down on the yellow sand.
The little waves cared not a bit,
But laughed aloud in glee,
Then smoothed their rumpled forms out.
And scampered back to sea.

(Sarah Chamberlain Weed)

译文

紧追不舍的赛跑

阳光灿烂,天空蔚蓝,
多么晴朗的一天。
风儿出现了,他深吸一口气,
说:"出来玩吧!"
小小浪花大声喊:
"等我们一起来玩游戏!"
然后迅速把他们的小白帽子,
系在他们长着酒窝的下巴颏儿底下。

"现在,"风儿大声喊,
"我们来赛跑,
看谁第一个跑到,
要跑得又快又远,
跑到黄色的沙滩终点线!"
小小浪花手拉手地跑,
一心想要得第一;
步伐坚定,呼吸急促,
风儿在后面紧紧追赶。

"哦!"浪花大声喊,
"我们赢了赛跑!
我们第一个跑到沙滩!"
"哈哈!"风儿笑了,然后把他们
全都推倒在黄色的沙滩上。
小小浪花一点儿也不在意,
反而高兴地大声笑,

然后抚平了他们弄皱的身躯,
蹦蹦跳跳地跑回了海洋。

（莎拉·张伯伦·威德）

练习

1. 抄写

Ruth was at Key West. Mark was at Key West. →
Ruth and Mark were at Key West.

_____

_____

2. 仿照上面的两个句子,改写下列的句子。

(1) A poor man sat at work. His wife sat at work.

_____

(2) Ulysses had been fighting at Troy. His soldiers had been fighting at Troy.

_____

(3) The little boys of Japan are gentle in manners. The little girls of Japan are gentle in manners.

_____

The Corn Song

Through valleys of grass and meadows of flowers,
Our plows their furrows made,
While on the hills the sun and showers
Of changeful April played.

We dropped the seed over hill and plain,
Beneath the sun of May,
And frightened from our sprouting grain,
The robber crows away.

All through the long, bright days of June,
The leaves grew green and fair,
And waved in hot midsummer's noon,
The soft and yellow hair.

And now, with autumn's moonlit eves,
The harvest-time has come,
We pluck away the frosted leaves,
And bear our treasure home.

There, richer than the fabled gift
Apollo showered from old,
Fair hands the broken grain shall sift,
And knead its meal of gold.

(John Greenleaf Whittier)

译文

玉米之歌

穿过溪边的草地和花田，
我们的犁杖留下了辙印。
山冈上时有阳光时有大雨，
多变的四月天气喜欢胡闹。

我们在山冈平原遍撒种子，
就在五月的太阳底下。
我们还从谷物的嫩芽旁边，
吓跑那群乌鸦强盗。

经过漫长而灿烂的整个六月，
叶子长得又绿又美丽。
在炎热的仲夏正午挥舞着的，
是柔软金黄的玉米须。

在秋天月光普照的前夕，
丰收的季节已经来临。
我们摘掉经霜的叶子，
将我们的财宝带回家里。

那里比童话里的礼物还要贵重，
太阳神曾抛洒许多金光。
勤劳之手筛起磨碎的谷粒，
碾出金黄色的谷粉。

（约翰·格林利夫·惠蒂尔）

Sweet and Low

Sweet and low, sweet and low,
Wind of the western sea,
Low, low, breathe and blow,
Wind of the western sea!
Over the rolling waters go,
Come from the dying moon, and blow,
Blow him again to me;
While my little one, while my pretty one,
Sleep.

Sleep and rest, sleep and rest,
Father will come to thee soon;
Rest, rest, on mother's breast,
Father will come to thee soon;
Father will come to his babe in the nest,
Silver sails all out of the west,
Under the silver moon:
Sleep, my little one, sleep, my pretty one,
Sleep.

(Alfred Tennyson)

译文

轻轻地，柔柔地

轻轻柔柔地，轻轻柔柔地，
西边来的大海的风，
柔柔地，柔柔地，呼吸着，吹拂着，
西边来的大海的风！

越过汹涌的潮水,
来自朦胧的月色,吹拂着,
再次把他带来给我;
当我的小宝贝,我漂亮的宝贝,
睡着时。

睡吧,休息;睡吧,休息,
父亲不久就会来到你身边;
休息吧,休息吧,在母亲的胸脯上,
父亲不久就会来到你身边。
父亲会来看他的宝宝,正在家里安睡,
从西方归来,扬起银色风帆,
在银色的月光下漂洋过海。
睡吧,我的小宝贝,睡吧,我漂亮的宝贝,
睡吧。

(阿尔弗雷德·丁尼生)

♠ 作者介绍

丁尼生年仅七八岁时,就在写字板上为哥哥写了他的第一首诗。"没错,你能写。"查尔斯这么说,事实确是如此。

在诗歌《花》中,丁尼生向我们展示了人们对其诗歌认知的看法,一开始称其为杂草,然后称其为花朵。他最伟大的诗歌包括《国王叙事诗》《加拉哈德》《伊诺克·阿登》《公主》和《悼念》等。

The Dream of the Boys

The sandman lost a dream one night ——
A dream meant for a boy;
It floated round awhile, and then,
It settled on a toy.

The toy dreamed that it stood in class
With quite a row of boys;
The teacher rapped upon his desk,
And cried, "Less noise! Less noise!"

Then looking at the toy, he scowled,
And said, "Next boy-foretell."
"Oh, please, sir," cried the little toy,
"I don't know how to spell.

"Indeed, I don't know how it is;
I am sure I am a toy,
Although I seem to be in class,
And dress up like a boy."

"What's that? What's that?" the teacher cried ——
In awful tones he spoke;
He came with strides across the floor,
And then the toy awoke.

There lay the nursery very still,
The shelf above it head;
The fire burned dimly on the hearth,
The children were in bed.

There lay the doll and Noah's Ark,
"Oh, dear me," said the toy,
"I just had such a dreadful dream!
I dreamed I was a boy."

(Catherine Pyle)

译文

男孩们的梦

某夜,精灵丢失了一个梦——
那梦属于一个孩童;
梦飘着,飘着,
最终落在了玩具的心中。

玩具梦见自己身处课堂,
站在一排又一排男孩旁;
老师的手轻轻地敲在桌上,
叫道:"不要吵,不要吵!"

接着,看向玩具,眉头紧锁地说:
"下一个男生——你来说说。"
"哦,求求你,老师。"孩子嗫嚅着,
"我不知道任何拼写的规则。"

"事实上,我不知道发生了什么事情。
我是个玩具,这点我可以肯定,
尽管我身处教室,
衣着打扮,像个孩子。"

"你说什么？你说什么？"老师大声咆哮——
这声音听起来不太妙；
老师大步流星，穿过走道，
接着，玩具惊醒，噩梦终止。

整个婴儿房内静悄悄，
头顶还是那个橱柜。
微弱的火光在壁炉里燃烧，
孩子们似乎仍在梦乡。

橱里的玩具还有玩偶和诺亚方舟。
"哎呀，吓死我了，"玩具开口说，
"我刚刚做了一个恐怖的梦！
我居然梦见自己变成了一个孩子！"

（凯瑟琳·派尔）

❀ 作者介绍

  凯瑟琳·派尔和她的兄弟霍华德·派尔（这位作者的其他作品见本套书第二册《美国语文——和小伙伴们在一起》）一样，不仅是诗歌艺术家，也是作家，他们都为孩子们写了大量的故事、诗歌，并且为这些故事配上了精美的插图。

Over the Hill

"Traveler, what lies over the hill?
Traveler, tell me.
I am only a child——from the window sill
Over I cannot see."

"Child, there's a valley over there,
Pretty and wooded and shy.
And a little brook that says, 'Take care,
Or I'll drown you by and by.'"

"And what comes next?"
"A little town, and a towering hill again.
More hills and valleys, up and down,
And a river now and then."

"And what comes next? "
"A lonely moor without a beaten way;
And gray cloud sailing slow before,
A wind that will not stay."

"And then?"
"Oh, rock and mountain and vale,
Rivers and fields and men,
Over and over repeat the tale,
And round to your home again."

(George MacDonald)

译文

山的那一边

"旅者,山的那一边是什么?
旅者,请告诉我。
我只是个趴在窗台边的孩子,
看不到山的那一边。"

"孩子,山的那边有座峡谷,
风景秀丽,树木林立,内敛娇羞;
还有小溪在轻声低吟:
'小心,不然我早晚会将你淹没。'"

"还有什么呢?"
"一个小镇,
小镇后面是一座高耸的山岭。
那里有更多的山丘和峡谷,连绵起伏,
间或有江河溪流经过。"

"还有呢?"
"一片寂静的荒原,
那里少有人走过;
还有慢慢划过天空的乌云,
风儿也不会停留。"

"还有呢?"
"哦,还有岩石、山巅和溪谷,
江河、田野和人们,
循环往复,生生不息,

绕了一圈之后,就又回到了你的家。"

（乔治·麦克唐纳）

♪ 作者介绍

乔治·麦克唐纳是一位作家,更是一位传教士。他著有短篇小说、长篇小说和诗歌。他的著作大部分是写给儿童的书,如《在北风的背后》《公主与柯迪》《仙女的日常》。麦克唐纳博士曾居于苏格兰和英格兰。

♪ 练习

1.读一读孩子的问题和旅行者的回答。

2.读诗的时候,你能分辨出这些话是谁说的吗?抄写最后两小节,删掉标点,并在每个问题和回答的段落前写下讲话者的身份。

Today

So here has been dawning
Another blue day;
Think, wilt thou let it
Slip useless away?

Out of Eternity
This new day is born;
Into Eternity
At night, will return.

Behold it before
No eye ever did;
So soon it forever
From all eyes is hid.

Here hath been dawning
Another blue day;
Think, wilt thou let it
Slip useless away?

(Thomas Carlyle)

 译文

今日

东方破晓，
又是晴朗的一天；
想想吧，
你要让它白白溜走吗？

从永恒之中，
新的一天诞生；
然后又回归永恒，
在夜晚降临的时分。

没有注意到今日的人，
就不会关注今日；
假如所有人都不重视今日，
就会永远忽视当下的力量。

东方破晓，
又是晴朗的一天；
想想吧，
你要让它白白溜走吗？

（托马斯·卡莱尔）

作者介绍

托马斯·卡莱尔是苏格兰最伟大的作家之一。他起初生活在爱丁堡，后来移居到了伦敦。他大多数的作品是历史散文和随笔，也创作了少量诗歌。

The Barefoot Boy

Blessings on thee, little man,
Barefoot boy, with cheek of tan!
With thy turned-up pantaloons,
And thy merry whistled tunes;
With thy red lip, redder still,
Kissed by strawberries on the hill;
With the sunshine on thy face,
Through thy torn brim's jaunty grace;
From my heart I give thee joy, ——
I was once a barefoot boy!
Oh, for boyhood's painless play,
Sleep that wakes in laughing day,
Health that mocks the doctor's rules,
Knowledge never learned in schools,
Of the wild bee's morning chase,
Of the wild flower's time and place,
Flight of fowl and habitude,
Of the tenants of the wood;
How the tortoise bears his shell,
How the woodchuck digs his cell,
And the ground-mole sinks his well;
How the robin feeds her young,
How the oriole's nest is hung;
Where the whitest lilies blow,
Where the freshest berries grow,
Where the ground-nut trails its vine,
Where the wood-grape's clusters shine.
Oh, for boyhood's time of June,
Crowding years in one brief moon,
When all things I heard or saw,

Me, their master, waited for.
I was rich in flowers and trees,
Humming-birds and honey-bees;
For my sport the squirrel played,
Plied the snouted mule his spade;
For my taste the blackberry cone,
Purpled over hedge and stone;
Laughed the brook for my delight,
Through the day and through the night—
Whispering at the garden wall,
Talks with me from fall to fall;
Mine the sand-rimmed pickerel pond,
Mine the walnut slopes beyond,
Mine, on bending orchard trees,
Apples of Hesperides!
Still as my horizon grew,
Larger grew my riches, too;
All the world I saw or knew.
Seemed a complex Chinese toy,
Fashioned for a barefoot boy!

(John Greenleaf Whittier)

译文

赤脚的男孩

祝福你，小小男子汉，
赤脚男孩，黝黑的脸蛋！
把裤脚高高挽起，
把快乐的口哨吹起；
你鲜红的嘴唇更加红润，

山上的草莓曾给你亲吻；
你的脸庞撒满阳光，
得意洋洋地展示受的伤；
我由衷地想让你快乐，——
我曾经也是赤脚男孩！
哦，童年是无忧无虑的嬉戏，
一觉醒来就是整天的欢笑。
健康得可把医生的规矩嘲笑，
知识不会比学校获得的少。
比如野蜂在清晨采蜜，
比如野花盛开在何时何地，
比如鸟儿飞翔，
比如林中万物的秘密。
乌龟是怎样背着它的壳，
土拨鼠是怎样挖着它的洞，
鼹鼠是怎样跌进井里；
知更鸟是怎样喂养幼仔，
黄鹂鸟是怎样筑巢。
还有哪里的百合开得最美，
哪里的浆果长得最鲜，
哪里的落花生拖曳着它的藤蔓，
哪里的野葡萄果实累累闪着光。
哦，童年的六月时光，
浓缩了多少岁月在其中，
我所听见、看见的一切，
待命于我这个它们的主宰。
鲜花绿树是我的财富，
鸟儿歌唱，蜜蜂酿蜜；
松鼠陪我玩游戏，
鼹鼠"吱吱"挖洞去。
黑莓长成我钟爱的模样，

紫色的果子爬满树篱和石墙；
小溪因我的快乐而欢笑，
日日夜夜，不息流淌——
在花园的墙边向我低语，
每个秋天和我交谈不停；
我那镶着一圈沙边的梭鱼池塘，
我那与天际相连的胡桃树山坡，
我那枝头弯弯的果树上，
满是金苹果园里的苹果！
我的视野还在扩展，
我的财富也在增加；
我所看见和熟悉的世界，
就像一个复杂的中国玩具，
专门为赤脚男孩量身定做！

(约翰·格林利夫·惠蒂尔)

✍ 作者介绍

约翰·格林利夫·惠蒂尔是贵格会成员，因此经常被称为"贵格诗人"。他出生于马萨诸塞州，大部分的人生在乡村度过。

在《赤脚男孩》这首诗里，惠蒂尔讲述了他童年生活的一些事情。从《学校生活》《脱壳机之歌》《雪域》和其他诗歌中也能看到他的早期生活。

A Simple Recipe

To be a wholly worthy man,
As you, my boy, would like to be,—
This is to show you how you can—
This simple recipe.
Be honest—both in word and act,
Be strictly truthful through and through
Fact cannot fail,—you stick to fact,
And fact will stick to you.
Be clean—outside and in, and sweep
Both hearth and heart, and hold them bright.
Wear snowy linen—aye, and keep
Your conscience snowy-white.
Do right, your utmost—good must come
To you who do your level best—
Your very hopes will help you some,
And work will do the rest.

(James Whitcomb Riley)

✍ 译文

简单的窍门

做一个令人尊敬的人,
我的孩子,因为你理应如此。
我会告诉你该怎么做,
有一个简单的法门。
要诚实——言行一致,
要彻彻底底地完全诚实。
真相最可贵——你要忠于真相,
真相也就会忠于你。

要干净——内外一致，
像清洁壁炉一样清洁心灵，让它们保持光亮。
穿洁白的亚麻衣服——永远，
让你的良心像雪一样白。
做正确的事，竭尽你的所能——正义一定会到来。
只要你全力以赴——
你的信心会给你帮助，
而剩下的只须努力就行。

（詹姆斯·惠特科姆·赖利）

作者介绍

詹姆斯·惠特科姆·赖利生活在印第安纳州，有"印第安诗人"之称。他为孩子们写了很多诗歌，如《童年的旋律》《儿童世界》和《快乐儿童之书》等。本诗选自1903年出版的《父亲的浪漫》，由出版商鲍勃·梅里尔公司特许授权。

阅读

Over his head were the maple buds,
And over the tree was the moon,
And over the moon were the starry studs,
That drop from the angel's shoes.

(Ralph Waldo Emerson)

译文

他头的上方是枫树的嫩芽，
枫树的上方是月亮，
而月亮的上方是从天使的鞋子上，
掉落下来的闪闪发光的星。

（拉尔夫·沃尔多·艾默生）

The Miller of the Dee

There dwelt a miller hale and bold,
Beside the river Dee;
He worked and sang from morn to night,
No lark more blithe than he;
And this the burden of his song,
Forever used to be,
"I envy nobody; no, not I,
And nobody envies me."

"You are wrong, my friend," said old King Hal.
"As wrong as wrong can be;
For could my heart be light as thine,
I'd gladly change with thee.
And tell me now, what makes thee sing,
With voice so loud and free?
While I am sad, though I'm the king,
Beside the river Dee?"

The miller smiled, and doffed his cap,
"I can earn my bread," quoth he.
"I love my wife, I love my friend,
I love my children three;
I owe no penny I cannot pay,
I thank the river Dee.
That turns the mill that grinds the corn,
To feed my babies and me."

"Good friend," said Hal, and sighed the while.
"Farewell! And happy be!
But say no more, if thou'dst be true,

That no one envies thee.
Thy mealy cap is worth my crown,
Thy mill my kingdom's fee;
Such men as thou are England's boast,
O miller of the Dee!"

(Charles Mackay)

译文

迪河边的磨坊主

有位健壮勇敢的磨坊主,
生活在迪河旁;
从早到晚工作,从早到晚歌唱,
云雀也比不上他欢乐;
他的歌是这样唱,
从来不曾改变:
"我不羡慕别人;不,我不羡慕,
并且也没有人羡慕我。"

"我的朋友,你错了。"年老的国王赫尔说,
"你大错特错;
因为如果我的心能像你的一样轻松,
我很乐意和你交换。
告诉我吧,什么让你歌唱,
歌声如此自在响亮?
我却如此悲伤,虽然我是国王,
生活在迪河旁。"

磨坊主笑着脱下他的帽子,

他说:"我能挣到面包,
我爱我的妻子,爱我的朋友,
爱我的三个孩子;
我不欠任何还不了的债,
我对迪河充满感激。
河水转动磨粉机碾碎玉米,
养活我的孩子和我自己。"

赫尔长久叹息,说:"好朋友,
再见!愿你一直快乐无比!
但是你错了,别再说没人羡慕你。
你那沾满面粉的帽子等同于我的王冠,
你的磨坊等同于我王国的封地;
你这样的人是英国的骄傲,
哦,迪河边的磨坊主!"

（查尔斯·麦凯）

作者介绍

查尔斯·麦凯博士出生于苏格兰。虽然麦凯写书并编辑报纸杂志,但他最为人所知的是歌曲。只要是说英语的地方,都在传唱他的《美好时光即将来临》《向西方!向西方!》和许多其他歌曲。

练习

1. 抄写

(1) Elizabeth was the queen of England.

(2) The leopard is found in Africa.

(3) Our sponges came from Key West.

(4) In South Carolina are great rice fields.

(5) The house was in Market Street.

Only One Mother

Hundreds of stars in the pretty sky;
Hundreds of shells on the shore together;
Hundreds of birds that go singing by;
Hundreds of bees in the sunny weather;

Hundreds of dewdrops to greet the dawn;
Hundreds of lambs in the purple clover;
Hundreds of butterflies on the lawn——
But only one mother in wide world over.

译文

只有一位大地之母

美丽的天空里星星无数；
沙滩上同时有贝壳无数；
歌唱着飞过的鸟儿无数；
晴朗的天气里蜜蜂无数；

向黎明问候的露珠无数；
紫色三叶草丛中羊羔无数；
草地上停着的蝴蝶无数——
但广袤世界却只有一位大地之母。

What the Wood-Fire Said

What said the wood in the fire,
To the little boy that night,
The little boy of the golden hair,
As he rocked himself in his little armchair,
When the blaze was burning bright?

The wood said, "See,
What they've done to me!
I stood in the forest a beautiful tree,
And waved my branches from east to west,
And many a sweet bird built its nest,
In my leaves of green,
That loved to lean,
In springtime over the daisy's breast.

"From the blossoming dells,
Where the violet dwells,
The cattle came with their clanging bells,
And rested under my shadows sweet,
And the winds that went over the clover and wheat,
Told me all that they knew,
Of the flowers that grew,
In the beautiful meadows that dreamed at my feet.

"And in springtime sweet faces,
Of myriad graces,
Came beaming and gleaming from flowery places;
And under my grateful and joy-giving shade,
With cheeks like primroses little ones played;
And the sunshine in showers,

Through all the bright hours,
Bound their flowery ringlets with silvery braid.

"And the lightning,
Came brightening,
From storm skies, and frightening.
The wandering birds that were tossed by the breeze,
And tilted like ships on black, billowy seas;
But they flew to my breast,
And I rocked them to rest,
While the trembling vines clustered and clung to my knees.

"But how soon," said the wood,
"Fades the memory of good!
For the forester came with his axe gleaming bright,
And I fell like a giant all shorn of his might.
Yet still there must be
Some sweet mission for me,
For have I not warmed you and cheered you to-night?"

So said the wood in the fire,
To the little boy that night,
The little boy of the golden hair,
As he rocked himself in his little armchair,
When the blaze was burning bright.

(Frank Stanton)

➢ 译文

柴火说了什么

那晚火堆里的木头,
有什么要对小男孩说?
当火焰熊熊地燃烧,
长着一头金发的小男孩,
在小小的扶手椅里摇啊摇。

木头说:"看看吧,
他们都对我做了些什么!
我本是一棵树,在森林里那么美丽,
我的枝条挥舞着从东又到西,
许多可爱的小鸟来搭巢,
就在我绿色的树叶里。
它们爱在春天的时候,
投进雏菊的怀抱去。

"牛儿从鲜花盛开的幽谷,
那紫罗兰的领地,
带着变幻的铃声,
来我可爱的树阴下休息。
风儿吹过苜蓿和麦子,
告诉我它们知道的消息。
花朵生长在美丽的草地,
而草地在我的脚下梦寐。

"春天到处是可爱的面庞,
快活欣喜地从繁华之地而来,

个个优美无比；
在我这令人愉悦的树阴里，
小家伙们脸若春花般地嬉戏；
阳光倾洒，
在整个明亮的白天里，
像银色的发带镶在他们美丽的卷发上。

"闪电来了，
光芒万丈，
穿过暴风雨的天空，令人恐慌。
漫游的鸟儿在狂风中飘摇，
像黑夜里汹涌海洋上的船；
但它们飞向了我的胸膛，
我摇晃着它们入眠。
当颤抖的藤蔓聚集起来，
也紧紧攀向我的膝盖。"

"然而没过多久，"木头说，
"美好的记忆就渐渐褪去！
因为伐木工带着他闪着寒光的斧子来，
我感觉自己像一个巨人却被剥夺了一切。
但肯定还有某样甜蜜的任务留给我，
难道我今晚没有令你温暖愉悦？"

那晚火堆里的木头，
这样对小男孩说。
当一头金发的小男孩，
在小小的扶手椅里摇呀摇，
火焰在熊熊地燃烧。

（弗兰克·斯坦顿）

练习

1. 抄写

(1) Did you notice how gamy he was, Little Brother?

(2) Oh, sister, look out of the window!

(3) Oh, mother, do get him some stockings and shoes!

(4) How do you do, David?

(5) Shove the boat in here, Joe!

(6) Can you tell me, Harry, where my knife is?

2. 看看上面的句子，你怎么知道这些话是对谁说的?

3. 找出五个带人名的句子。

Ring Out, Wild Bells

Ring out, wild bells, to the wild sky,
The flying cloud, the frosty light.
The year is dying in the night;
Ring out, wild bells, and let him die.

Ring out the old, ring in the new,
Ring, happy bells, across the snow,
The year is going, let him go;
Ring out the false, ring in the true.

(Alfred Tennyson)

译文

响吧,狂野的钟

响吧,狂暴的钟,向着狂野的天空,
向着乱舞的云彩,向着冰冷的寒光。
这一年即将在今夜逝去;
响吧,狂暴的钟,就让他消亡。

声声辞旧岁,声声迎新年,
响吧,幸福的钟,响彻皑皑白雪,
这一年即将过去,就让他过去吧;
在钟声中去伪存真。

(艾尔弗雷德·丁尼生)

练习

1.把这首诗里押韵的单词写下来。_____

My Country, 'tis of Thee

My country, 'tis of thee,
Sweet land of Liberty,
Of thee I sing,
Land where my fathers died,
Land of the Pilgrims' pride;
From every mountain-side,
Let Freedom ring!

My native country thee,
Land of the noble free,
Thy name I love;
I love thy rocks and rills,
Thy woods and templed hills;
My heart with rapture thrills,
Like that above.

Let music swell the breeze,
And ring from all the trees,
Sweet Freedom's song;
Let mortal tongues awake;
Let all that breathe partake;
Let rocks their silence break,
The sound prolong.

Our fathers' God, to Thee,
Author of Liberty,
To Thee we sing;
Long may our land be bright,
With Freedom's holy light:
Protect us by Thy might,

Great God, our King!

(Samuel F. Smith)

译文

祖国之歌

我的祖国，属于你，
可爱的自由城邦，
我为你歌唱，
祖先们在此安眠，
朝圣者为此骄傲。
在每一个山腰，
响起自由的号角！

我的祖国，
崇高的自由城邦，
我是多么爱你；
我爱你的岩石和溪水，
你的森林和建有神庙的山峰；
我的心充满狂喜的颤动，
爱你所有的一切。

让风中充满音乐，
在所有的林中吟唱，
甜蜜的自由之歌；
让人类的语言觉醒；
让所有的生灵分享；
让巨石打破它们的沉默，
歌声久远悠长。

我们的天父，
自由的创造者，
我们为你歌唱；
愿我们的祖国永远辉煌，
闪耀着自由神圣的光芒；
请用你的强大保佑我们，
伟大的上帝，我们的国王！

（塞缪尔·F. 史密斯）

The Rock-a-by Lady

The Rock-a-by Lady from Hushaby Street,
Comes stealing; comes creeping;
The poppies they hang from her head to her feet,
And each hath a dream that is tiny and fleet——
She brings her poppies to you, my sweet,
When she finds you sleeping!

There is one little dream of a beautiful drum——
"Rub-a-dub!" it goes;
There is one little dream of a big sugar-plum,
And lo! thick and fast the other dreams come,
Of popguns that bang, and tin tops that hum,
And a trumpet that blows!

And dollies peep out of those wee little dreams,
With laughter and singing;
And boats go a-floating on silvery streams,
And the stars peek-a-boo with their own misty gleams,
And up, up, and up, where the Mother Moon beams,
The fairies go winging!

Would you dream all these dreams that are tiny and fleet?
They'll come to you sleeping;
So shut the two eyes that are weary, my sweet,
For the Rock-a-by Lady from Hushaby street,
With poppies that hang from her head to her feet,
Comes stealing; comes creeping.

(Eugene Field)

译文

摇篮夫人

摇篮夫人从乖乖睡大街来，
蹑手蹑脚，悄悄走来；
从头到脚挂满罂粟花，
每朵都有一个微小易逝的梦想——
她带她的花儿给你，我亲爱的，
就在你沉沉入睡之际。

一面美丽的鼓是一个小小的梦想，
它总是"咚咚咚咚"响；
一颗大糖果也是一个小小的梦想。
瞧，其他的梦想接二连三地来，
有"砰砰砰"的玩具枪和"嗡嗡嗡"的罐头盖，
还有吹起来的小喇叭"嘀嘀嘀嘀"响。

洋娃娃在那些很小的梦里出现，
欢声笑语，不停歌唱。
小船在银色的溪水上飘荡，
星星和自己迷蒙的亮光捉迷藏。
向上，向上，向上，在月亮妈妈微笑的地方，
小精灵张开翅膀到处飞翔！

你做过所有这些微小又易逝的梦吗？
当你沉睡之时他们就会来到你身旁；
所以闭上疲倦的眼睛，我亲爱的，
因为摇篮夫人从乖乖睡大街来，
从头到脚挂满罂粟花，

蹑手蹑脚，悄悄走来。

（尤金·菲尔德）

✿ 作者介绍

尤金·菲尔德出生于圣路易斯，晚年生活在芝加哥，并于1895年辞世。菲尔德先生非常喜爱孩子，并为他们创作了许多美妙的作品，无人能望其项背。

他最受欢迎的诗歌包括《小男孩布卢》《小蓝鸽》和《云肯、布林肯和诺德》等。本文选自《童年的爱之歌》，由查尔斯·斯克里布纳家族出版公司于1899年出版。

The Gladness of Nature

Is this a time to be cloudy and sad,
When our mother Nature laughs around;
When even the deep blue heavens look glad,
And gladness breathes from the blossoming ground?

There are notes of joy from the hang-bird and wren,
And the gossip of swallows through all the sky;
The ground-squirrel gaily chirps by his den,
And the wilding bee hums merrily by.

The clouds are at play in the azure space,
And their shadows at play on the bright green vale,
And here they stretch to the frolic chase,
And there they roll on the easy gale.

There's a dance of leaves in that aspen bower,
There's a titter of winds in that beechen tree,
There's a smile on the fruit, and a smile on the flower,
And a laugh from the brook that runs to the sea.

And look at the broad-faced sun, how he smiles,
On the dewy earth that smiles in his ray,
On the leaping waters and gay young isles;
Ay, look, and he'll smile thy gloom away.

(William Cullen Bryant)

译文

大自然的喜悦

这怎会是发愁悲伤的时刻?
当我们的自然之母笑声响彻;
深蓝色的天空也满是喜悦,
繁荣的大地洋溢欢乐的气息。

悬巢鸟和鹪鹩唱出快乐的音符,
燕子叽叽喳喳的声音响彻天空;
地松鼠在它的洞穴旁欢快地叫,
而野蜜蜂兴高采烈地"嗡嗡"飞过。

云朵在蔚蓝的天空里游戏,
影子投映在明亮的绿色溪谷里。
在这边伸展身体追逐嬉戏,
在那边翻滚在舒适的微风里。

杨树林里叶子在起舞,
山毛榉里风儿在欢笑,
果实在欢笑,花儿在欢笑,
奔流入海的小溪在欢笑。

看太阳的那张大脸,笑得多爽朗,
露水滋润的大地在它的光芒里微笑,
翻腾的海水和年轻的岛屿扬起欢乐的笑容;
哎,看哪!它的笑容让你远离忧伤。

(威廉·卡伦·布莱恩特)

作者介绍

威廉·卡伦·布莱恩特小时身体虚弱,无法正常地上学读书。他在家跟私人教师学习,通过这种方式获得教育考上大学。

Whippoorwill Song

Let down the bars; drive in the cows,
The west is barred with burning rose.
Unhitch the horses from the plows,
And from the cart the ox that lows,
And light the lamp within the house:

The whippoorwill is calling,
"Whippoorwill, whippoorwill,"
Where the locust blooms are falling
On the hill!

The sunset's rose is dying,
And the whippoorwill is crying,
"Whippoorwill, whippoorwill,"
Soft, now shrill,
The whippoorwill is crying,
"Whippoorwill."

(Madison Cawein)

译文

夜鹰之歌

打开栅栏,赶进牛群;
西边燃烧着玫瑰色的云。
马儿卸下了犁杖,
"哞哞"叫的牛儿卸下车厢,
屋子里四处灯火明亮:

北美夜鹰在呼号,
"呜呜喔喔,呜呜喔喔。"
那里槐花飘零,
落满山冈!

夕阳的玫瑰光芒渐渐消逝,
北美夜鹰不停呼号,
"呜呜哦哦,呜呜哦哦,"
从轻柔到尖厉,
北美夜鹰不停呼号,
"呜呜哦哦,呜呜哦哦。"

(麦迪逊·凯万)

The Prayeth Best

Farewell, farewell! But this I tell
To thee, thou wedding-guest:
He prayeth well, who loveth well
Both man and bird and beast.

He prayeth best, who loveth best,
All things both great and small;
For the dear Lord, who loveth us,
He made and loveth all.

(Samuel Taylor Coleridge)

译文

最好的祷告

再见了,再见!但我得对你说,
各位来婚礼上贺喜的客人,
要想祷告最有效,就要好好爱所有,
无论人类或鸟兽。

要想祷告最有效,就要好好爱所有,
无论是大还是小。
因为亲爱的上帝爱着我们,
他创造所有又热爱所有。

(塞缪尔·泰勒·柯勒律治)

Selection

Do not look for wrong and evil,
You will find them if you do.
As you measure to your neighbor,
He will measure back to you.

Look for goodness, look for gladness,
You will meet them all the while;
If you bring a smiling visage,
To the glass, you meet a smile.

(Alice Cary)

译文

选段

不要追寻错误和恶行,
一旦你找了就会找到它们;
就像你揣测你的邻居,
他也同样会揣测你。

去追寻善良和快乐,
如此你终将与它们相遇;
若你带一张微笑的面庞给玻璃,
你也将会与微笑相遇。

(爱丽丝·卡里)

Bob White

There's a plump little chap in a speckled coat,
And he sits on the zigzag rails remote,
Where he whistles at breezy, bracing morn,
When the buckwheat is ripe, and stacked is the corn,
"Bob White! Bob White! Bob White!"

Is he hailing some comrade as blithe as he?
Now I wonder where Robert White can be!
Over the billows of gold and amber grain,
There is no one in sight——but, hark again,
"Bob White! Bob White! Bob White!"

Ah! I see why he calls; in the stubble there,
Hide his plump little wife and babies fair;
So contented is he, and so proud of the same,
That he wants all the world to know his name:
"Bob White! Bob White! Bob White!"

(George Cooper)

译文

一只叫鲍勃·怀特的鹑鸟

那里有个穿着花外套的小胖家伙，
远远坐在弯弯曲曲的铁轨上，
在微风轻送、令人振奋的清晨吹起口哨，
彼时荞麦已经成熟，玉米硕果累累，
"鲍勃·怀特！鲍勃·怀特！鲍勃·怀特！"

他是在向某个如他一般快乐的小伙伴打招呼吗？
我现在好奇罗伯特·怀特究竟会在哪儿！
越过金色的麦浪和琥珀色的谷穗，
看不见任何人——但是，我又听见了：
"鲍勃·怀特！鲍勃·怀特！鲍勃·怀特！"

啊哈！我明白他为什么喊了。
在那边的割完的麦茬里，
藏着他胖乎乎的妻子和孩子；
他是如此满足，也是如此自豪，
想让全世界都知道他的名字：
"鲍勃·怀特！鲍勃·怀特！鲍勃·怀特！"

（乔治·库珀）

✑ 作者介绍

　　乔治·库珀写的最有趣的诗歌都是关于鸟儿、植物和户外生活的。《风和叶》《秋》和《鸟儿的回归》是其中最为有名的几首。

The Toadstool

There's a thing that grows by the fainting flower,
And springs in the shade of the lady's bower;
The lily shrinks, and the rose turns pale,
When they feel its breath in the summer gale,
And the tulip curls its leaves in pride,
And the blue eyed violet starts aside;
But the lily may flaunt, and the tulip stare,
For what does the honest toadstool care?

(Oliver Wendell Holmes)

译文

毒蘑菇

长在渐渐枯萎的花朵边,
生在女子闺房的阴影里。
百合缩成一团,玫瑰花容失色,
当夏日微风送来它的气息,
郁金香傲慢地卷起叶片,
蓝眼睛的紫罗兰跳去一边;
但百合也许到处夸耀,郁金香呆呆盯着瞧,
老实的毒蘑菇可没什么好计较。

(奥利弗·温德尔·霍姆斯)

作者介绍

人们有时会叫奥利弗·温德尔·霍姆斯博士"独裁者",这个外号出自他《早餐桌上的独裁者》一文。他出生于波士顿。

Chater 7

History and Biography | 历史与自传

预习

boundary /ˈbaʊndri/ 边界
colony /ˈkɑːləni/ 殖民地
companion /kəmˈpæniən/ 同伴
congress /ˈkɑːŋɡrəs/ 议会
determined /dɪˈtɜːrmɪnd/ 决断的
influence /ˈɪnfluəns/ 影响
license /ˈlaɪsns/ 执照
measurements /ˈmeʒəmənts/ 测量
painstaking /ˈpeɪnzteɪkɪŋ/ 辛苦的
persevering /ˌpɜːrsəˈvɪrɪŋ/ 坚韧的
quarrel /ˈkwɔːrəl/ 争执
rebellious /rɪˈbeljəs/ 反抗的
scorching /ˈskɔːrtʃɪŋ/ 烧伤的
surveyor /sərˈveɪər/ 调查者

The Young Surveyor

On a stream in Virginia in the days when Virginia belonged to the English, there stood a plain little school-house that was known as the Bridges Creek School. Among the boys that used to say their lessons there, were a tall blue-eyed boy named George, the son of a widow, who lived not far from the school.

George was the sort of boy that not only teachers but other boys liked very much. When he studied, he studied hard; and when he played, he played hard. He was large and strong, and excelled all his schoolmates in mud. Ding and leaping and throwing.

One very likable thing about him was his fairness. Though he was only fourteen years of age, the other boys used to bring him their quarrels to settle because he could always tell who was in the wrong. Besides being fair, he was honest and manly. He had a way also of persevering in everything that he tried to do, whether it was working a hard sum in arithmetic, or riding a bucking horse.

He was careful and painstaking in all his school work but the study that he took most interest in was surveying. From this he was learning how to measure land, and how to show the boundaries of estates and farms. He had decided to become a surveyor.

He made surveys all over the neighborhood, and kept regular books in which he entered boundaries and measurements as carefully as if they belonged to real surveys instead of being school work He left school before he was sixteen; but he went right on with his study of surveying, and when he was sixteen he was given a surveyor's license.

A surveyor was of great importance in those days, because there were many Virginians who had large tracts of land the boundaries of which had to be fixed.

One of these Virginia landowners was a man named Lord Fairfax, whose lands reached beyond the Blue Ridge Mountains. He often visited Georges brother, Lawrence, at Mount Vernon, Lawrence's beautiful home on the Potomac River, and used to meet George there.

He was a queer old gentleman, but he learned to like George very much. This was not surprising, for George's manners were modest and frank and pleasing. As soon as the young surveyor received his license, Lord Fairfax decided to give him a chance to do some real Surveying.

In company with a young kinsman of Lord Fairfax's he was sent out to make a survey of the Fairfax lands beyond the Blue Ridge. It was his first journey into the great wilderness, and it was full of interest to him.

There was snow on the mountain tops when the young travelers first set out, but spring was not far away. They rode through thick forests, and over high mountains into a vast and beautiful valley, beside a river that the Indians called "the daughter of the stars".

One night a band of Indians came upon the surveying party, and George had a chance to see an Indian war dance. Up to this time he had not much to do with Indians, but he thought it likely that he should have to deal with them often in his business, so he watched them closely, as they whooped and yelled and twisted and turned.

About two weeks had passed in a wild country in the mountains, where the work of making the survey was carried on. Most of the time the young surveyors camped out, living on wild turkeys and other game. Each had to be his own cook; chips of wood had to serve for dishes.

One day the wind was so strong that their tent was blown down; another time they were driven out by smoke; another time by rain; and one night the straw on which George was sleeping caught fire, and he was awakened by his companion just in time to escape scorching.

At last the work was finished and George returned home and made his report to Lord Fairfax. His lordship was greatly pleased with what had been done, and used his influence to get George appointed as public surveyor.

That was the first public officer that the young surveyor ever held. But it was by no means the last. While he was still a very young man, he was in command of important movements against the French and Indians, who were fighting with the English for the Ohio Valley.

When the English were at last successful, the young commander returned to Mount Vernon. This was now his own property, for his brother Lawrence had died and willed it to him.

After some years trouble came to Virginia and to all the other English colonies in America. England, the mother country, began taxing the Americans unjustly, and they began to rebel against the injustice.

The English king determined to put down the rebellious spirit of the colonists. In vain did the Americans try to get their rights by petition to the king. There was nothing left for them to do but to take up arms against the mother country.

The Congress of the Colonists asked the master of Mount Vernon to leave his pleasant home, where he had lived for fifteen happy years, and to become the commander-in-chief of the American army. He agreed to do so.

Perhaps you may have read how he led that army, through terrible sufferings and bitter defeats to final victory over the English.

Perhaps you have read, too, that when peace was declared he became the first president of the United States of America, the nation that he had done so much to make. Perhaps you know that to this day the name of the young surveyor is the greatest name in American history, the name of George Washington.

(Rose E. Young)

译文

年轻的测量员

从弗吉尼亚被英国人占领的那一天起，弗吉尼亚州的一条小溪旁就伫立着一个普通的小校舍，大家都称之为桥湾学校。在校的众多学生中，有一个个子高高、蓝色眼睛的男孩子，名字叫乔治。乔治的妈妈是一个寡妇，他们家住在离学校很远的地方。

乔治是那种很受欢迎的学生，不仅老师们宠爱他，其他的男孩子们也很喜欢他。他总是学得认真，玩得尽兴。乔治长得高高壮壮，在跑步、跳高、投铅球等运动中，表现也远远超过其他学生。

在乔治身上，有一种很值得欣赏的品质，就是公正。虽然乔治只有十四岁，但其他孩子总是让乔治来评判他们之间的争执，因为他们相信乔治一定会正确地评判出谁错谁对。乔治不仅公平，而且诚实，做起事来像个小男子汉。不管是做数学运算时，还是驾驭跳脱的马驹时，他都能以坚韧不拔的毅力完成自己参与的各种事情。

学校里面的所有功课，乔治都能够认真努力地去学习。其中，他最感兴趣的就是测量课。在测量课上,乔治学会了如何去丈量土地,如何计算庄园和农场的边界。他想成为一位测量员。

乔治在学校周边进行各种调查,定期记录测量的数据,如房屋的边界和大小。他不仅把测量当作学校的功课,更是把它当作真正的测量来做。乔治十六岁离开学校后,仍然继续从事测量工作,并在当年就获得了测量资格证。

在那个时代,测量的作用重大。许多弗吉尼亚人拥有大片的土地,这些土地的边界亟待确定下来。

弗吉尼亚当地有一个地主叫费尔法克斯勋爵,他拥有的土地跨越蓝岭山脉。他经常去弗农山地区拜访乔治的哥哥劳伦斯。劳伦斯美丽的家就坐落于波托马克河旁边。在劳伦斯家里,费尔法克斯勋爵见到了乔治。

费尔法克斯勋爵是一个性格古怪的老绅士,但是他渐渐喜欢上了乔治。这并不是什么奇怪的事情,因为乔治态度谦逊,仪态大方,令人愉悦。乔治一拿到测量资格证,费尔法克斯勋爵就决定给乔治一个机会,让乔治从事真正的测量工作。

乔治接到任务,和费尔法克斯勋爵的一个亲戚一起开展对费尔法克斯蓝岭山脉地区土地的丈量工作。这是乔治第一次到大荒原进行测量,他觉得兴致勃勃。

当年轻的测量员开始工作的时候,山顶还有积雪,但是春天已经快来到了。他们跨越茂密的森林,爬过高耸的山脉,进入宽阔秀美的山谷。山谷就在一条河边,印第安人把这条河称为"星星的女儿"。

一天晚上,一群印第安人碰到了测量队,乔治因此有机会欣赏到了印第安人的战阵舞。在此之前,乔治一点也不了解印第安人,但是一想到自己以后经常要与他们打交道,乔治开始仔细观察起那些正在喊叫着、扭动着跳舞的印第安人。

两个星期过去了,在广阔的大山中行进的日子还在继续。大部分的时间,年轻的测量员们要在野外露营,抓野生的火鸡吃,开展一些其他的活动。乔治需要自己动手煮饭,亲自用碎木屑生火。

有一次强风将他们的帐篷吹倒,有一次他们被浓烟熏了出去,还有一次他们被雨水淋湿。有一天晚上,乔治正在睡觉,他帐篷下面的铺草着火了。幸好乔治的同伴及时赶到叫醒乔治,乔治才能免于被火烧伤。

最终,测量任务顺利完成,乔治回到家中,撰写出测量报告交给费尔法克斯勋爵。费尔法克斯勋爵对乔治的报告非常满意，于是他利用自己的影响力，帮助乔治成了正式的测量员。

这是这位测量员第一次担任公职。但这并不是故事的结局。过了几年，乔治还很年轻的时候，他领导了一场群众运动，对抗法国人和印第安人，与英国人一起并肩战斗，争夺俄亥俄河谷。

英国人最终胜利了。胜利之后，乔治回到了弗农山。弗农山此时已经是他私人的财产了，因为他的哥哥去世，他继承了哥哥的财产。

许多年后，弗吉尼亚地区，以及其他的英属美国殖民地区遇到了新的问题。英国，他们的母国，开始对美国人征收大量的赋税，人民开始反对这种不公正的政策。

英国国王试图把殖民地的反抗情绪镇压下去。殖民地的美国人在向英王请愿无效的情况下，不得不拿起武器保卫自己的国家。

殖民地议会请求弗农山的主人离开他住了十五年的美丽家乡，出任美国军队的总司令。他答应了。

也许你曾在书本上读到过他如何领导这支军队，度过艰难岁月，经历过痛苦的失败，最终打败了英国人。

也许你还读到过，当战争结束后，他成了美国，这个让他为之奉献与奋斗的国家的第一任总统。也许你已经知道这位年轻的测量员的名字，这是一个美国历史上最伟大的名字——乔治·华盛顿。

（罗斯·E.杨）

Doing His Best

Luke Varnum was fifteen years old when many of the boys and all the men of the village in which he lived shouldered their guns in 1776, and marched off to war. Luke was lame; so he was left at home. With a heavy heart, he saw the others march away. It was hard not to go with them.

Perhaps he thought bitterly of his lameness and felt that one who could not be a soldier was of no use in the world. We shall see if he thought rightly.

The men had been gone an hour and a half, when three horsemen galloped up to the door of the village blacksmith's shop.

"Halloo!" said one, "is there any one here who can set a shoe?"

"I think I can," said Luke. "I often tend the fire for Jonas, and have seen him do it."

Luke started up the bellows and soon had a bright fire. He found a few nails which Jonas had left and made two more himself. Just at this point a fourth horseman appeared, walking his horse slowly toward the shop.

"I see that you have found a forge," he said, as the others saluted him. "It is well for my horse, for I could not ride it five miles farther unshod."

Luke pared the horse's hoof and measured the shoe. He found it too large. He heated it white and bent it to the proper size. Then he nailed it on and, for pride's sake, used first the two nails which he had made himself.

"It isn't done very well, I know," he said, "but I have done my best, and I think the shoe will do."

"It will do very well," said the rider, " and without it, my horse would be useless."

He then mounted his horse, and rode away with the soldiers, but one of them lingered a minute and said to Luke, "Boy, no ten men can serve their country so well today as you have done. The rider of that horse is Colonel Warner."

When you read some day in books of history how Colonel Warner reached the battle-field of Bennington with his regiment just in time to save the day, you must remember Luke Varnum.

He did what he could, and, although it was a little thing, yet it helped to gain a great victory.

(Elihu Burritt)

译文

尽己所能

1776年的时候,卢克·瓦纳姆才15岁。当时,村里所有的男人和大多数男孩都扛上了枪,离开家前往战场。卢克的腿脚不好,被迫留在了家里。他心情沉重,只能眼睁睁看着其他人行军离开。不能和他们一起上战场保卫家园真是太让人难受了!

可能是他把瘸腿这件事想得太过严重了,觉得一个不能成为战士的人在这个世界上毫无用处。不过,这个想法是否正确,我们很快就会明白。

大部队离开一个半小时后,三个人骑马疾驰,来到村子里的铁匠铺。

"哈罗!"一个人打招呼,"这里有谁能钉马掌吗?"

卢克回答说:"我想我能,我经常帮乔纳斯照料炉火,我见过他钉马掌。"

卢克开始拉风箱。风箱发出了巨大的轰鸣声,很快,明亮的火焰就燃了起来。他找到了一些乔纳斯留下的钉子,自己又做了两枚。就在这时,第四个人出现了。他牵着他的马,慢慢地朝着铁匠铺走来。

先来的三个人看见了他,都向他致意,他回应道:"我看见你们找到了一个铁匠铺。这真是太好了,如果不给我的马钉上马掌的话,我恐怕只能骑着它跑上八千米。"

卢克修剪了马蹄,测量了蹄铁,结果发现它对于马掌来说太大了。于是他将蹄铁煅烧成白色,把它弯曲成合适的尺寸,然后钉到了马掌上面。老天哪,他用的是先前自己做的两枚钉子。

"我知道我做的不是太好。"他说,"但我已经尽力了,我想蹄铁会起作用的。"

那名骑马人回答说:"你做得很好,要不是你,我有马也没用。"

接着他跨上马鞍,和战士们一起疾驰而去。不过,他们中有一个人稍微逗留了一会儿,他对卢克说:"小伙子,你今天为国家做了最大的贡献。刚才那匹马上的骑士是华纳上校。"

当你有一天读到历史书的时候,你一定会对卢克·瓦纳姆这个名字留下深刻印象。因为就在那天,华纳上校带领一个团的兵力及时抵达了本宁顿战区,扭转了整个战局。

虽然只是很小的一件事,但卢克尽力了,同时也为国家赢得了伟大的胜利。

（伊莱休·伯里特）

♪ 作者介绍

伊莱休·伯里特,出生于康涅狄格州,常被人称为"知识渊博的铁匠"。他很小的时候就当上了一名铁匠。但他非常喜爱学习,把自己所有的业余时间都用在了读书上。他经常一边工作,一边摊开书阅读。他精通多种语言,写了不少好书,其中有《铁砧上的火花》和《多层芯片》。

The Return of Columbus to Spain

The return of Columbus from the New World was a great event in the little port of Palos. At least one member of almost every family had been with him.

As soon as the sails of Columbus's ship were seen in the harbor, all the people began to rejoice. Bells were rung, shops were shut, and all business was stopped.

Columbus landed and walked in procession to the Church of St. George to return thanks to God for his safe arrival. The air rang with shouts, and great honor was everywhere paid to him.

In a few days, King Ferdinand and Queen Isabella sent for him to come to Barcelona. The journey of Columbus to this city was like that of a king. Wherever he passed, all the people poured out to see him.

In the large towns, the streets, windows, and balconies were filled with persons. Everybody was eager to gain a sight of him and of the Indians that were with him. The Indians were gazed upon with as much wonder as if they had come from another planet.

It was about the middle of April when Columbus arrived at Barcelona and the weather was delightful. He entered the city in triumph.

First were paraded the six Indians, painted and wearing ornaments of gold. After these were carried live parrots, and stuffed birds and animals of unknown kinds, and strange plants.

After this, Columbus followed on horseback, and with him were many Spanish nobles and knights. The streets were filled with people, and the houses were crowded even to the roofs.

To receive Columbus properly, the king and queen had ordered their throne to be placed in public, under a rich canopy of cloth of gold. There they awaited his arrival, seated in state, with their son Prince Juan beside them.

Presently, Columbus arrived, looking very stately and commanding. On his approach, the king and queen arose, as if receiving a person of the highest rank. Columbus bent his knees, and would have kissed their hands as a subject, but they raised him in the most gracious manner and ordered him to seat himself in their presence. This was a rare honor.

He now gave an account of the most striking events of his voyage, and showed them the Indians and the products that he had brought from the New World.

When Columbus had finished, the king and queen sank on their knees, and poured forth thanks and praises to God. All the people did the same thing; and there was everywhere present a deep and solemn gladness that prevented any noise of triumph.

(Washington Irving)

译文

哥伦布返航西班牙

对于小港口帕洛斯来说，哥伦布从新世界返航是一件很重大的事情。这里几乎每家都有一个人和他一起出航。

哥伦布船队的白帆刚刚出现在港口，人们就立刻开始欢呼起来。钟声敲响，商店歇业，一切事务都停下来。

哥伦布上岸后，走在一列队伍中，他走进圣乔治大教堂，为他的安全抵达而感谢上帝。空气里满是兴奋的呼喊，每个地方都满载着人们对他的敬意。

几天后，国王费迪南德和王后伊莎贝拉召他来巴塞罗那觐见。一路上，哥伦布得到了国王般的待遇。不论他走到哪里，所有人都倾巢而出，只为了看他一眼。

在那些大城镇里，街道、窗台和露台上都挤满了人。每个人都急切地盼望着，希望能被他和那些随行的印第安人看上一眼。人们用惊奇的眼光盯着印第安人，就好像他们是从另一个星球来的。

哥伦布抵达巴塞罗那的时候，正是四月中旬。天气晴朗，令人愉快。他怀着胜利的喜悦进入了城门。

走在最前面的是六个印第安人，他们涂脂擦粉，挂满金子做的装饰品。紧跟着他们的一行人带着活鹦鹉、鸟类标本、不知名的动物以及古怪的植物。

然后，哥伦布骑在马背上出场了。许多西班牙贵族和骑士围绕在他身边。街上挤满了人。道路两边的房子里，甚至屋顶上都挤满了人。

为了欢迎哥伦布的到来，国王和王后下令把他们的王座安置在公开场合，王座上方竖起了一个奢侈的金色华盖。他们庄严地坐着，等待哥伦布的到来。他们的儿子胡安王子陪坐在一旁。

哥伦布很快就到来了，看上去庄重而威严。他一到，国王和王后就立刻站了起来，仿佛是在接待一位地位最高的人。哥伦布深深地屈身行礼，正打算要亲吻他们的手，但他们用最亲切仁慈的态度命令他起身，并让他坐了下来。这可真是罕有的荣誉。

随后，他讲述了那些发生在航行途中引人入胜的事件，并向他们展示印第安随从和他从新世界带回来的战利品。

当哥伦布讲完后，国王和王后跪倒在地，倾诉他们对上帝的感谢和赞美。于是所有人都跪下祷告，每一处都洋溢着深沉而威严的喜悦，最终取代了凯旋的喧嚣。

（华盛顿·欧文）

Columbus

Behind him lay the gray Azores,
Behind the Gates of Hercules;
Before him was not the ghost of shores,
Before him only shoreless seas.
The good mate said, "Now must we pray,
For lo! the very stars are gone.
Brave Admiral, speak, what shall I say? "
"Why, say, Sail on! Sail on! And on !"

(Joaquin Miller)

✍ 译文

哥伦布

暗淡的亚述尔群岛在他身后,
隐身于赫尔克里斯之门;
他的前面没有幽灵般的海岸,
只有无边无际的海洋。
那个一流水手说:"让我们祈祷,
因为星星已然消逝。
勇敢的上将啊,我们该说些什么?"
"哎呀!起航!起航!起航!"

(华金·米勒)

Sir Walter Scott's Dogs

Sir Walter Scott loved dogs, and looked upon them as good friends. When Washington Irving was paying Scott a visit, they went one morning for a walk.

As the gentlemen started, every dog in the house turned out to go with them. First of all came the old hound Maida. He was a noble animal, and Scott loved him the best of all.

Hamlet was a young black greyhound that had not yet grown wise.

There was also a beautiful setter, with soft silken hair, long drooping ears, and mild eyes. She was Mrs. Scott's pet.

From the kitchen came still another greyhound, hailed by Scott as an old friend and comrade.

Maida walked ahead. He was very quiet, as though he wished to show that he knew how to behave himself.

The young dogs did not mind his manner. They wanted some fun. They would play about him, leap on his neck, worry his ears, and try to tease him into a frolic.

For a long time Maida would keep on, only now and then seeming to give his young friends some advice. At length he would make a sudden turn, seize one of them, and tumble him in the dust.

Then he would glance at the gentlemen, as much as to say, "You see, I can't help giving way to this sport."

After that he would jog on as before. Scott laughed at Maida. "I make no doubt," he said, "that when Maida is alone with these young dogs, he plays the boy as much as any of them."

Pretty soon the dogs found something that set them to barking. It was some time before Maida would join them, but at last he opened his mouth with a very loud "Bow-wow"!

Then he wagged his tail, and looked into his master's face to see if it was right.

"Yes, yes, old boy!" cried Scott. "You did wonders. You shook the hills with your roaring. You may now lie your guns by for the rest of the day."

(Washington Irving)

译文

沃尔特·司各特爵士的狗

司各特爵士很爱狗，他把狗狗们当作自己的好朋友。有一次，华盛顿·欧文去拜访司各特，司各特正和狗狗们在一起散步。

这位绅士每走一步，屋子里的每一只狗都紧紧地跟着他。为首的是老猎犬梅达，他是一只血统纯正的猎犬，司各特最喜欢他。

哈姆雷特是一只年轻的黑色格雷伊猎犬，他还没有被驯化得很聪明。

还有一只美丽的塞特犬，她的毛犹如丝绸般柔软，长长的耳朵耷拉着，眼神温和。她是司各特夫人的宠物。

厨房里又跑出来一只格雷伊猎犬，他是司各特的老朋友和好伙伴。

梅达走在最前面，他非常安静，好像要表示自己知道如何守规矩。

年轻的狗狗们则丝毫不在意礼貌问题，他们只想找乐子。他们会和司各特胡闹，往他的脖子上跳，在他的耳边吵吵闹闹，并且还想和他玩。

梅达继续往前走，可是，他这会儿似乎想给这些年轻的朋友们一点教训。他突然转身，抓住其中一只，把他按到地上。

然后，他看了一眼那些"绅士"们，好像在说："看吧，在这项运动上，我还是当仁不让的吧！"

之后，他又恢复了原先的小跑步伐。"毫无疑问，"司各特嘲笑梅达说，"梅达和他们在一起的时候，和他们中的任何一个一样，都是个顽皮的小男孩。"

很快，狗狗们发现了什么东西，叫了起来。梅达没有叫，但是，过了一会儿，梅达也张开了嘴巴，大声地"汪汪"叫了起来。

然后他摇了摇尾巴，望向主人的脸，想来看看自己做的对不对。

"好，好，老朋友。"司各特嚷道，"你创造了奇迹呀！你的咆哮响彻整座山，今天剩下的时光，你就别叫啦。"

（华盛顿·欧文）

作者介绍

独立战争结束前,华盛顿·欧文出生在纽约,"虽然华盛顿已经实现了他的伟业,"他的母亲欧文夫人说,"但我的孩子应当以他的名字命名,表示对他的纪念。"

欧文长大成人之后,去了英国生活,并在那里待了很多年。也是这个时期,他拜访了沃尔特·司各特爵士,这个故事收录在《见闻札记》里。这本书中还包括《瑞普·凡·温克尔》和《睡谷的传说》等篇目。

华盛顿·欧文还写了许多其他书。比如《阿尔罕布拉》《华盛顿的一生》和《哥伦布的一生》等。

The Boy That Was Hired Out

When Michael Angelo was twelve years old, he did a piece of work that greatly pleased the painter Ghirlandajo. Although Michael had not been taught by anyone, the artist declared that here was a lad of genius, who should become a painter.

This is what the little boy most wished to do, but he had no hope that his father would for a moment listen to the plan.

Michael's father, Ludovico, was a great man in the state, but thought little of art and artists. He wished his son to become a statesman, and this Michael well knew.

Ghirlandajo was so eager to teach the boy, however, that he went in company with Michael to visit his father. The artist then asked Ludovico to place Michael in his studio.

"I wish my son to become a great man in the state, not a dauber and a mason," said Ludovico, who was very angrily. When he found how earnest Michael was, however, he gave way.

He would not say that he was willing to place his son with Ghirlandajo. He would not admit that the study of art was a study, or that the studio of an artist was anything but a shop.

At last he said to Ghirlandajo, "I give up my son to you. He shall be your servant or anything you please for three years, and you must pay me twelve dollars for his services ."

In spite of the insulting words and the insulting terms, Michael Angelo agreed. He was thus hired out as a servant to the artist, whom his father should have paid for teaching him.

Nor was this all. Michael had to suffer much, indeed, in addition to the anger of his father. His fellow-pupils were jealous of his great genius, and they constantly ill-treated him.

Three years passed away, and Michael was still the pupil of Ghirlandajo. One day the boy went to the Gardens of St. Mark, where there was a great and costly museum of art works. This museum had been established by Prince Lorenzo, who was the foremost friend of art in the city of Florence.

One of the workmen in the garden gave the boy permission to try his hand at copying some of the marble figures there. Michael had studied only painting. He was glad of a chance now to try the chisel, which he preferred to the brush.

He chose for his model an old figure of a faun, which was a little spoiled. The mouth, indeed, was broken off, but this did not trouble the boy.

Day after day the boy worked at the piece. From his own fancy, he made a new mouth for it, with the lips parted in laughter and the teeth showing.

When Michael had finished; and was looking at his work, a man standing near asked if he might offer a criticism.

"Yes," answered the boy, "if it is a just one."

"Of that you shall be the judge," said the man.

"Very well, what is it?"

"The forehead of your faun is old, but the mouth is young. See, it has a full set of perfect teeth. A faun as old as this one is would not have perfect teeth."

The lad admitted the justice of the criticism. At once he chipped away two or three of the teeth; and chiseled the mouth so as to give it aged look.

The next morning when Michael went to remove his faun from the garden, it was gone. He searched long for it; but without success. Finally, seeing the man who had spoken about the teeth, he asked him if he knew where it was.

"Yes," replied the man, "and if you will follow me, I will show you where it is."

"Will you give it back to me? I made it and have a right to it."

"Oh, if you must have it, you shall."

With that he led the way into the palace of the prince, and there, among the most precious works of art, stood the faun. Michael cried out in alarm, "Prince Lorenzo will never forgive the fact that such a piece of work has been brought among his treasures of art."

To his astonishment, the man declared that he was the Prince Lorenzo himself, and that he set the highest value upon this work. "I am your friend," he added, "and you shall be counted as my son. You are also certain, to become one of the great masters of art."

This was great good fortune. Prince Lorenzo was a powerful nobleman, known far and wide to be an excellent judge of works of art. His approval was in itself fame and fortune.

Filled with joy, the lad went straightway to his father's house, which he had been forbidden to enter. Forcing his way to Ludovico, Michael told him what had happened. The father refused to believe the good news until he was led before Prince Lorenzo.

The prince, by way of showing his good-will, then offered Ludovico any post that he might choose. The statesman asked for only a modest place.

"It is good enough," he said, "for the father of a mason."

(George Cary Eggleston)

译文

租来的男孩

米开朗基罗十二岁时完成了一幅画，这幅画让画家吉兰达伊奥大为赞赏。尽管他还没有跟任何人学过绘画，但这位艺术家断言这个少年很有天赋，将会成为画家。

这正是这个小男孩最企盼的事了，但他不指望父亲能花点时间听听这个想法。

米开朗基罗的父亲洛多维科是政府里的大人物，根本瞧不起艺术和艺术家。米开朗基罗也非常明白父亲希望自己成为一名政治家。

吉兰达伊奥很想教这孩子画画。他亲自陪米开朗基罗去见他的父亲，请求他把儿子送进自己的画室。

洛多维科十分气愤地说："我希望我儿子成为这个国家里的大人物，而不是什么涂鸦者或者泥瓦匠。"但当他发现米开朗基罗是多么热衷于此时，终究还是让了步。

他并不乐意把儿子交给吉兰达伊奥，也不把学习艺术看成一项正经的学习，认为艺术家的工作室只不过是一家商店而已。

最终他对吉兰达伊奥说："我不要这个儿子了，把他交给你。接下来的三年里，你可以把他当作仆人来使唤，你想让他做什么都行，但你必须给我十二美元作为报酬。"

米开朗基罗没有理会这些侮辱性的话，同意了这些条件。于是，他被租给画家充当仆人，而按常理，他父亲本该付钱让自己的孩子接受教育。

这还没完，除了忍受父亲的怒火，米开朗基罗还遭受了很多苦难。一同学习的人都嫉妒他的天才，对他很不友善。

三年过去了，米开朗基罗仍然是吉兰达伊奥的学生。一天，这个男孩去了圣马可花园，那里有座造价不菲的大艺术博物馆。这座博物馆是佛罗伦萨最有名的艺术之友，洛伦佐大公建立的。

花园里的一位工作人员允许这个孩子试试身手，仿制那里的大理石像。米开朗基罗只学过绘画，但很高兴有机会用一用凿子，这种工具比起画刷更让他感兴趣。

他选了一座略有破损的老农牧神雕像当模特。雕像的嘴部已经损坏，但这难不倒他。

他在这东西上忙了一天又一天，凭着自己的想象，给它雕了一个全新的、微笑着张开双唇、露出牙齿的嘴巴。

米开朗基罗完成了他的作品，凝视着它。这时，有位站在一旁的先生询问是否能够提点批评意见。

"可以，"男孩回答说，"只要你的意见合理就行。"

"这将由你来决定。"那个男士说道。

"那好，什么样的意见？"

"你那农牧神的前额已显老态，但嘴巴却是年轻的样子。你看，它有一副完好无缺的牙齿，一个如此年迈的农牧神不该有这样整齐的牙齿。"

少年承认这个批评很合理。他马上动手凿去了两三颗牙齿，重新雕刻了嘴部，让它给人一种年迈的感觉。

　　第二天早晨，米开朗基罗打算把他的农牧神雕像搬离花园，却发现它已不知去向。他花了很长时间到处寻找，可一无所获。最后，他看到了那位和他谈论牙齿的男子，问他是否知道雕像到哪儿去了。

　　"是的，我知道，"那位先生回答，"跟我来，我让你看看它在哪里。"

　　"你能把它还给我吗？它是我做的，理应属于我。"

　　"哦，如果你一定要取回它，当然可以。"

　　他带着他走进了大公的宫殿，而农牧神像正伫立在那些最珍贵的艺术作品之中。米开朗基罗惊慌地大叫起来："洛伦佐大公是绝不会容忍这样粗鄙的作品和他那些艺术瑰宝放在一起的。"

　　让他震惊的是，那位男子表示自己就是洛伦佐大公，并高度肯定了这一作品。"我是你的朋友，"他补充道，"你也可以算作是我的孩子，你一定会成为一名艺术大师。"

　　这是一笔巨大的财富。洛伦佐大公不仅是一位很有权势的贵族，还是一位见多识广的艺术品鉴赏大师。他的认同本身就代表了名望和财富。

　　少年满心欢喜，直奔父亲的屋子。此前父亲不准他进家门。米开朗基罗硬是挤到了洛多维科的身边，告诉他发生了什么。他父亲直到被带到洛伦佐大公跟前，才相信这个好消息是真的。

　　大公为了表达他的好意，告诉洛多维科他想当什么官都可以，而这位政府官员只选了一个不起眼的职位。

　　"对于一个泥瓦匠的父亲来说，这已经足够了。"他说道。

（乔治·加里·艾格斯顿）

✍ 作者介绍

　　艾格斯顿先生曾在美国的西部、南部和北部生活过，他写过美国的许多地方。他和兄弟爱德华·埃格尔斯顿儿时在印第安纳的生活被记录在《最后的平底船》和《第一个印地安纳人》这两本有趣的书中。

　　《被租来的男孩》选自《历史上的奇事》一书。1885年这本书由哈珀兄弟出版公司出版。

A Southern Officer to His Boys

Ship Massachusetts, off Lobos, February, 27, 1847.

My dear Boys:

I received your letters with the greatest pleasure, and, as I always like to talk to you both together, I shall not separate you in my letters, but write one to you both.

You will learn, by my letter to your grandmother, that I have been to Tampico. I saw many things to remind me of you, though that was not necessary to make me wish that you were with me. The river was calm and beautiful, and the boys were playing about in boats, and swimming their ponies.

Then there were troops of donkeys carrying water through the streets. They had a kind of saddle, somewhat like a cart-saddle, though larger, that carried two ten-gallon kegs on each side, which were a load for a donkey.

The donkeys had no bridles on, but would come along in strings to the river and as soon as their kegs were filled; start off again. They were fatter and sleeker than any donkeys that I had ever seen before, and seemed to be better cared for.

I saw a great many ponies, too. They were larger than those in the upper country, but they did not seem so hardy. I got one to ride around the fort and walls.

This pony had a Mexican bit and saddle on, and paced delightfully, but every time my sword struck him in the flanks, he would jump and try to run off. Several of them had been broken to harness by Americans, and I saw some teams, in wagons, driven four-in-hand, well matched and trotting well.

We had a grand parade on General Scott's arrival. The troops were all drawn up on the bank of the river, and fired a salute as he passed them.

He landed at the market, where lines of sentinels were placed to keep off the crowd. In front of the landing the artillery was drawn up, which received him in the center of the column, and escorted him through the streets to his lodgings.

They had provided for him a handsome gray horse, with rich harness, but General Scott preferred to walk, with his staff around him, so a dragoon led the horse behind us. The windows along the streets we passed were crowded with people, and the boys and girls were in great glee. The Governor's Island band played all the time. There were six thousand soldiers in Tampico.

I think that you would have enjoyed with me the oranges and sweet potatoes. Major Smith became so fond of the chocolate; that I could hardly get him away from the house. We remained there only one day.

I have a nice state-room on board this ship; Joe Johnston and I occupy it, but my poor Joe is so sick all the time that I can do nothing with him.

I left Jem to come on with the horses, as I was afraid that they would not be properly cared for. Vessels are fitted up for the horses, and parties of dragoons are appointed to take care of them.

I do not think that we shall remain here more than one day longer. General Worth's and General Twigg's divisions have arrived. These include the regulars, and I suppose that the volunteers will be coming on every day.

We shall probably go on the first down the coast, select a place for debarkation, and make all the arrangements for the arrival of the troops.

I shall have plenty to do there, and am anxious for the time to come. I hope that all may be successful. Tell Rob that he must think of me very often, be a good boy, and always love papa. Take care of Speck and the colts.

Mr. Sedgewick and all the officers send their love to you. Be sure that I am thinking of you, and that you have the prayers of your affectionate father.

Robert E. Lee

译文

一名南部军官写给儿子们的信

我亲爱的孩子:

很高兴收到你们的信。我一向喜欢跟你们两个同时说话,写信也不例外,这封信写给你们两个人好了。

你们看了我写给祖母的信,就会知道我到过坦皮科。在那里看到的许多事物都使我想起你们,虽然并不希望你们与我同来。那里河流平静美丽,孩子们乘着船玩耍,让小马在河里游来游去。

那时有成队的驴子驮着水穿过街道。他们身上装着鞍鞯,这种鞍鞯有点像运货鞍,不过要更大些,两边各挂着两个四十升的水桶,这分量对于驴子来说可是不轻。

这些驴子没有套笼头,但却能鱼贯而行。走到河边,装满水桶,他们就再度返回。他们比我见过的驴子更加肥壮,油光水滑,似乎被饲养得更周到。

我还看到了许许多多的小马。坦皮科的小型马比内陆马体型更大,但好像并没有那么强壮。我弄了匹马,骑着他游览了堡垒和城墙。

这匹马配有墨西哥式的嚼子和马鞍,跑起来姿势优美,但每次我的佩剑戳到他的肚子,他就跳起来想逃跑。这样的小马有一些已经被美国人驯服,我看到几支马车队伍,都是用四匹马拉车。马儿很听话,一路小跑。

斯科特将军来时,我们举行了盛大的阅兵。全体人员列队站在河岸,在将军经过时鸣枪致意。

将军上岸的地方是市集,那儿站了几行卫兵阻拦人群。码头前面排着火炮队迎接将军,护送他到住处。

他们给将军准备了一匹鞍具齐全的灰色骏马,但将军想和随行人员一同步行,于是由一名骑兵牵着马跟在我们旁边。我们走过的街道,两边的窗户都有许多人在张望,男孩女孩们兴高采烈。总督岛乐队一直奏乐。坦皮科有六千名军人。

我觉得你们一定跟我一样喜欢坦皮科的橘子和红薯。史密斯少校爱上了那里的巧克力,我简直没法把他拖到房子外面去。我们只留了一天。

我在船上的住处相当不错，是跟乔·约翰斯顿同住一间高级包房。然而可怜的乔一直晕船，我无计可施。

我担心别人照顾不好我们的马，就离开杰姆去看马。安置马的舱室专门布置过，一队骑兵受命照看马匹。

我觉得我们最多在这里待一天。沃思将军和特威格将军的军队都到了，正规军就是这些，我想志愿军每天都会来一批。

也许我们要率先下船，选个地方，为军队登陆做好一切准备。

我会有很多事情要做，现在焦灼地等待着。我希望一切顺利。告诉罗布，叫他多想着爸爸，做个好孩子，而且要一直爱爸爸。照顾好斯佩克和小马驹。

赛奇威克先生及全体军官向你们致以爱意。爸爸想念你们，满怀爱意地为你们祈祷。

R. E. 李

1847年2月27日

于从洛沃斯启程的马萨诸塞号上

（罗伯特·李）

作者简介

罗伯特·李在弗吉尼亚出生，曾在西点军校受训，父亲是在美国独立战争中有"小马哈利"之名的亨利·李将军。墨西哥战争中，罗伯特在司各特将军的军队中担任总工程师，就是这时写下了这封给儿子们的信。

1861年，弗吉尼亚州脱离联邦，罗伯特认为自己应当辞去职务，与弗吉尼亚共进退。不久，他便成了北弗吉尼亚同盟军司令。

南北战争后，罗伯特·李将军担任了位于弗吉尼亚州列克星敦的华盛顿学院（现名华盛顿与李大学）校长。

Cadet Grant at West Point

In the winter of 1838-1839, I was attending school at Ripley (only ten miles distant from Georgetown), but spent the Christmas holidays at home. During this time my father received a letter from the Honorable Thomas Morris, then United States Senator from Ohio.

When he read it, he said to me, "Ulysses, I believe that you are going to receive the appointment."

"What appointment?" I inquired.

"To West Point; I have applied for it."

"But I won't go," I said.

"I think that you will." And I thought so too, even if my father did.

Besides this argument in favor of my going to West Point, there was another strong reason. I had always a great desire to travel. Going to West Point would give me the chance to visit the two great cities, Philadelphia and New York.

This was enough. When these places had been visited, I would have been glad to have a steamboat or railroad accident happen, or any other accident, in fact, by which I might have received a slight injury. What I wished was, not to have to enter the Academy. Nothing of the kind occurred, and I had to face the music.

A military life had no charms for me, and I had not the faintest idea of staying in the army, even if I should be graduated. The encampment, which came before the commencement of studies, was very tiresome.

When the 28th of August came——the date for breaking into camp and going into barracks——I felt as though I had been at West Point always, and that if I stayed till graduation, I should have to remain always. I did not take hold of my studies with eagerness, but I could not sit in my room doing nothing.

There is a fine library connected with the academy. From this cadets can get books to read in their quarters. I devoted more time to these than to the books relating to the course of studies.

Much of the time, I am sorry to say, was spent on novels, but not those of a trashy sort. I read all of Bulwer's then published, Marryat's, Scott's, Washington Irving's works, and many others.

Mathematics was very easy to me, so that when January came, I passed the examination, taking a good standing in that branch. In French, the only other study at that time in the first year's course, my standing was low.

In fact, if the class had been turned the other end first, I should have been near the head. I never succeeded in getting squarely at either end of my class in any one study, during the four years.

During my first year's encampment, General Scott visited West Point, and reviewed the cadets. With his commanding figure, great size, and showy uniform, I thought him the finest-looking man that my eyes had ever beheld, and the most to be envied.

I could never resemble General Scott in appearance. But I believe that I did have a feeling for a moment that some day I should occupy his place on review, although I had no thought then of remaining in the army.

At last all the examinations were passed. The members of the class were then called upon to name their choice of arms of service and regiments. I was anxious to enter the cavalry, or dragoons, as they were then called. (There was only one regiment of dragoons in the army at that time, and attached to that, besides the complement of officers, there were at least four brevet second lieutenants.) I put down, therefore, my first choice, dragoons; second, infantry; and got the latter.

Having made first and second choice of two different arms of service, with different uniforms, I could not get a uniform until I knew which place I was to have. Notice did not reach me for several weeks. Then it took at least a week to get a letter to the tailor, and two more to make the clothes and have them sent to me. During all this time I was very anxious.

Soon after the arrival of the clothes, two things happened which gave me a great dislike for military uniform.

A few days after the suit came, I put it on, and went to Cincinnati on horseback. I rode along a street of that city, imagining that everyone was looking at me, with a feeling akin to mine when I first saw General Scott.

A little urchin, bareheaded, barefooted, with ragged trousers held up by a single suspender, seeing me, cried. "Soldier! Will you work? No, sir-ee; I'll sell my shirt first!"

The other circumstance occurred at home. Opposite our house in Bethel stood the old stage tavern, where man and beast found shelter. The stableman drank a good deal, but he possessed a sense of humor.

On my return I found him parading the streets, and attending in the stable, barefooted, but in a pair of sky-blue trousers, just the color of my uniform trousers, with a strip of white cotton sheeting sewed down the outside seam in imitation of mine.

The joke was a huge one in the minds of many people, and was much enjoyed by them; but I did not like it so well.

(Ulysses S. Grant)

译文

尤里西斯在西点军校

1838年到1839年的冬天，我在里普利（离乔治敦不过一万六千米）上学，但在家中度过了圣诞假期。那时，父亲收到了托马斯·莫里斯的来信，这位可敬的先生后来成了俄亥俄联邦的参议员。

读信时他对我说："尤里西斯，我相信你会得到任命。"

"什么任命？"我询问道。

"去西点军校；我已经为此提出了申请。"

"但我不想去。"我回答。

"我认为你应该去。"如果父亲这样认为，我想也只能照做了。

除了这次争辩，还有另一个重要原因促使我去西点军校。我非常渴望旅行，去西点军校就相当于获得了参观费城和纽约这两座美妙城市的机会。

这些理由足以让我动身了。等我游历完这些地方以后，我很乐意遇上一起汽船、火车或者别的什么事故，兴许我还会因此受到轻伤，只要我不用进学校就行。但这样的事情没有发生，我不得不面对现实。

军旅生涯对我来说一点吸引力都没有。即便我从学校毕了业，也丝毫不会想留在军队。学习正式开始之前的露营生活已经让我烦透了。

8月28日，我被迫进了军营的那一天，我感到仿佛我已经在西点军校过了一辈子，而如果继续在这里读到毕业，说不定我一辈子都得耗在这儿。我无法对学习投入热情，但也不想总坐在屋中无所事事。

学院旁有座不错的图书馆，学员们可以从那里找点书在宿舍里读读。相比和课程有关的书，我在这些书上花了更多的时间。

很遗憾，我把许多时间用来读小说了，不过不是那些垃圾东西。我读了布尔沃那时已出版的所有小说，还有马里亚特、斯科特、华盛顿·欧文以及很多别的作家的作品。

数学对我来说很容易，所以一月我通过了考试而且名列前茅。至于法语，第一学年中唯有这门课我没有取得好成绩。

事实上，如果课程看重其他方面的能力，我应该能名列前茅。在四年中，我从来没有碰到过能让我完全发挥能力的学科。

在我第一年宿营期间，斯科特将军视察西点军校并检阅了学员。目睹了他那威严的仪态、健硕的身躯以及炫目的制服后，我认为他真是我见到过的最帅气、最让人羡慕的人。

我的长相和斯科特将军没法比，但我在那刻闪过一个念头。即便我当时并不想留在军队，但我却相信总有一天会在检阅仪式中充当他那样的角色。

通过了所有的考试后，班级里的学员要填报志愿，选择军种团队。我很想加入骑兵部队，也就是那时所说的龙骑兵。（那时军中只有一个龙骑兵团，这个兵团除了有军官的编制，还有至少四名荣誉少尉的名额。）于是，我写下了我的志愿，第一是龙骑兵，第二是步兵。结果我被分配到了后一个团队。

由于我第一志愿和第二志愿分属两个军种，制服样式不同，于是不得不等到去向明确后才定做制服。我是几周后才接到通知的，又花了至少一星期才联系到裁缝，随后他又花了两周时间才交货。在这期间我一直焦躁不安地等待着。

服装送到后不久发生了两件事情，让我极为讨厌军装。

收到制服的几天后，我穿上它骑着马去了辛辛那提。在城市的大街上骑马而过时，我幻想众人看到我的心情，就和我第一次见到斯科特将军一样。

一个没戴帽子、光着脚、穿着邋遢裤子的小捣蛋鬼拿着简陋的托架,他看到我便大声道:"大兵!能帮个忙吗?哦,不,先生;让我先卖了我的衬衣!"

还有一次是在我的老家。在我们贝塞尔的屋子对面有座老旧的供旅人歇脚的酒馆。来来往往的有各色人等,还有各种牲畜。那里有位马夫嗜酒如命,但他还挺有幽默感。

在我回去的路上,看到他在街上昂首步入马棚。他光着脚,却穿着和我制服裤子同色的天蓝色裤子。还效仿我的制服,把长条白棉布缝在外侧的裤缝上。

这个玩笑在很多人的脑海中留下了深刻的印象,他们对这件事乐此不疲,而我却感到不太自在。

(尤里西斯·辛普森·格兰特)

作者介绍

尤里西斯·辛普森·格兰特是美国第十八任总统。《西点军校时期的格兰特学员》取自《格兰特将军回忆录》这本书,在书中格兰特将军讲述了他一生的故事。他在美墨战争中担任中将,并在后来的美国内战中成了联邦军总司令。

Chief John Marshall

John Marshall was one of a large family of children. Their father was not a rich man, and when John was a boy it was not easy to get the comforts of life. The father made up his mind, however, to send his children to school.

No doubt in after years John thanked him many times for this schooling. Nor would he ever regret the hardships by which he gained what made him the great and good man that he was.

You may be sure that he, like other little boys and girls, was often tired of his books, but he did not give up because of that.

As John Marshall grew older, there was no office in the gift of his country that he could not have had. When he died he was greatly mourned, and it was felt that in his death the country suffered serious loss.

He was very poor, and often had to dress shabbily. When he lived in Richmond, he used to go to market with his basket on his arm, and bring home what was needed.

One day he was turning away from the market with his purchases, when he heard a young man near him speaking harshly. Marshall turned and saw a finely dressed young man, who had bought a turkey and who could not find any one to carry it home for him.

"Of course I cannot take it home myself," said the young man. "What am I to do?" And he was very angry at the bare idea.

John Marshall stepped up to him, and said quietly, "Where do you live, sir?"

The young man turned, and seeing a shabbily dressed old countryman, thought, "This old fellow wants to make a little money, so I shall let him carry my turkey. "Handing over the turkey, the young man said, "You may follow me."

Judge Marshall did so. When they reached the end of their walk, the young man took the turkey, and handed the bearer a piece of money. The young man was astonished when it was declined, and said to someone passing, "Who is that curious old fellow?"

"That is Judge Marshall, Chief Justice of the United States," was the answer.

You may imagine how the young man felt as he said, "What made him bring home my turkey?"

"Perhaps to give you a lesson on false pride," was the answer.

(Mary Tucker Magill)

译文

大法官马歇尔

约翰·马歇尔出生在一个大家庭，家里孩子很多。他的父亲不是一个有钱人，所以约翰小时候的日子并不那么好过。虽然生活艰苦，但父亲还是决定送孩子们去上学。

无疑，在这之后的许多年，约翰为能够上学而感谢了父亲许多次。他从不后悔自己付出的那些艰苦努力，他从中获益匪浅，最终成了一个伟大的人，成了一个好人。

像其他孩子一样，约翰也常常会厌倦那些无穷无尽的功课，但他从没有搁下自己的学业。

约翰·马歇尔年岁渐长，表现也越来越出色。国家系统中，没有他应征不到的职位。他死后，人们深切地悼念他，认为他的离世使得整个国家蒙受了巨大的损失。

约翰生活清贫，经常穿着破旧的衣服。他在里士满的时候，经常会在胳膊上挎着个篮子去市场采购生活必需品。

一天，他买好了东西正准备离开市场，却听到身边有一位年轻人怒气冲冲地说着什么。马歇尔转过身，见到一名穿着体面的年轻人，他买了一只火鸡，却没人帮他把火鸡送回家去。

这名年轻人抱怨道："我不能亲自把它拿回去，这是肯定的。我该怎么办？"他无计可施，感到非常恼怒。

约翰·马歇尔走过去轻轻地问他:"先生,你住在哪儿呢?"

那名年轻人转过身,看到的是一个穿得破破烂烂的乡下老人,他想:"这个老家伙想要赚点钱,我应该让他帮我送火鸡。"他把火鸡递过去,说:"跟我来。"

马歇尔法官照做了。他们到达目的地,年轻人拿回了火鸡,给了这名搬运工一块钱。但这个老人谢绝了,年轻人感到非常惊讶,问一名过路人说:"这个奇怪的老头是谁?"

"约翰·马歇尔,美国的大法官。"

年轻人问:"为什么他要帮我把火鸡送回家?"你能想象到这时他心里的感受吧?

结果得到的答案是,"我想是他要给你一个教训,让你懂得不要妄自尊大"。

(玛丽·塔克·马吉尔)

✿ 作者介绍

这个故事选自《维吉尼亚名人》一书。马吉尔女士在这本书里讲述了许多关于德高望重的人的有趣故事。

Chapter 8
Stories of Kids | 儿童故事

🎧 预习

disappointment /ˌdɪsəˈpɔɪntmənt/ 失望
dollar /ˈdɑːlər/ 美元
eager /ˈiːgər/ 热切的
education /ˌedʒuˈkeɪʃn/ 教育
geography /dʒiˈɑːgrəfi/ 地理
paddle /ˈpædl/ 桨
physical /ˈfɪzɪkl/ 天然的
recess /rɪˈses/ 休息
rueful /ˈruːfl/ 后悔的
stern /stɜːrn/ 船尾
study /ˈstʌdi/ 学习
whistle /ˈwɪsl/ 吹口哨

Cotton(1)

When Albert Wise was twelve years old, his father let him go from his home in New York to visit his uncle in Georgia.

In the villages and country through which he passed, he saw many things that were new and strange. But nothing seemed stranger or more beautiful than the fields of cotton, which he saw from the cars, as they rolled swiftly on through the cotton-growing region.

He had seen cotton on the docks in the harbor of New York, but never before had he seen it growing. He was glad to think that he should learn all about it while on his uncle's plantation.

The first morning after his arrival, he begged his uncle to take him into the cotton-fields.

It was the middle of September, and the fields were white with the fleecy staple. Albert was delighted. There were long rows of plants about three feet high, bearing pretty blossoms, some cream-colored, some pink; and a kind of pod or "boll," as it is called, from which the fluffy cotton was bursting forth.

Men, women, and children were hard at work picking the soft white locks from the bolls, and putting them into bags that hung at their sides.

"Now, Albert, you see how cotton grows, and how it is picked. This kind of work is very different from the mowing and raking of hay that you have seen so much in the North."

"Indeed it is," said Albert. "I think I should never tire of such work as this. It is real fun," he said, as he drew a lock of cotton from one of the open bolls.

"Yes, Albert, it is fun for you now, but soon the sun will make it very warm here, and then you will not think it such fun. But people who are used to the hot sun of the South do not seem to mind it very much."

When Albert had enjoyed the sport of cotton-picking for a while, he was glad enough to go with his uncle to finish their talk in the shade of the fine old oak that stood in front of the house.

"What do you find besides the cotton?" his uncle asked, as Albert was tearing open a lock of cotton which he had brought from the field.

"Ever so many little black seeds," replied Albert, "and see, uncle, how the cotton sticks to them. How do you get it off?"

"That is done by a machine called a cotton-gin, Albert. Once it had to be done by hand, and then it took a long time to get enough cotton to make a pair of trousers.

"The cotton-gin does the work very quickly. It has a great many round saws about the size of a dinner plate. These are made to go round very fast. They have hundreds of fine sharp teeth, which catch hold of the cotton and tear it from the seed.

"The gin was invented many years ago, by Eli Whitney, who lived near Savannah; but the gins which we have now are much better than the first that were made."

"I should like to see a gin," said Albert.

"You shall," replied his uncle. "You can see the gin-house from here, on the other side of the fields. Someday soon I will take you there when the gin is at work."

译文

棉花（1）

当艾伯特·怀斯12岁的时候，他父亲就让他离开在纽约的家，去探望他那在格鲁吉亚的叔叔。

走过这个国家的村落，他长了不少见识。但是，这些地方再神奇，再美丽，也不如他们横穿这片长着棉花的地区时，他从车上看到的棉花地。

他在纽约港口那些船坞上见过棉花，但是从没见过正在生长的棉花。他高兴地想，自己应该在叔叔的农场里彻底了解这种植物。

刚到农场的头一天早上，艾伯特就央求叔叔带他去棉花地。

正值9月中旬，田地里是羊毛般又轻又白的农作物。艾伯特欣喜不已。这些长排的植物有一米高，顶着可爱的花骨朵儿，有粉色的，也有米白色的。松软的棉花是从豆荚，准确地说，是从"圆荚"里冒出来的。

男人们、女人们还有孩子们都在忙于劳作，把那些柔软的白色的芯子从圆荚里摘出来，放进他们挂在身体两侧的袋子里。

"好了，艾伯特，你看到棉花是怎么长、怎么摘的了。这样的活儿和你在北方看到的收割和耙拉干草完全不一样吧。"

"确实是，"艾伯特说，"我觉得我永远都不会厌倦像这样的工作。这实在是太有趣了。"他说着，把棉芯从一个开口的圆荚里扯出来。

"是的，艾伯特，现在你觉得很有意思，但这里很快就会被晒热，那时候你就不会觉得有意思了。不过，这对已经习惯南方的烈日的人们来说，倒是没什么大不了的。"

等艾伯特玩够了采棉花的游戏后，才兴高采烈地和叔叔一起，来到房屋前那棵茂盛的老橡树下，在树荫里继续聊天。

"除了棉花，你还发现了什么？"他的叔叔问，艾伯特正在拆一团他刚从地里带来的棉花芯。

"还发现了这些黑色的小籽儿，"艾伯特回答道，"你看，叔叔，棉花籽粘得很紧，你怎么把它们弄掉？"

"那是由一台叫作轧棉机的机器完成的。艾伯特，要是需要人工来做的话，做一条裤子都会要花很久才能得到足够的棉花哩。

"轧棉机工作起来很快，它有非常多的圆轮，看起来大概一个晚餐盘的大小，它们的运转速度非常快。机器里有几百个锋利的齿轮，可以缠住棉花，然后把棉花从籽儿中绞下来。

"而轧棉机，是伊莱·惠特尼在很多年前发明的，他就住在萨凡纳附近。但我们现在使用的轧棉机比第一台轧棉机要好多了。"

"我想看看轧棉机。"艾伯特说。

"你会看到的，"他的叔叔答道，"从这儿你就能看到轧棉房，在田地的另一边。过不了几天，等轧棉机工作的时候，我就带你去。"

Cotton(2)

"There must be a great many seeds from such large cotton-fields, uncle. What becomes of them all?"

"The finest will be kept for planting next year, but most of them will be sold to the oil-mills. There they are put into a press, and the oil is squeezed from them.

"A hard cake is left in the press. This is ground into meal, which the planters use for feeding cattle and for fertilizing the cotton-fields.

"Cotton-seed oil is one of the most valuable articles of commerce."

"Does the cotton plant ever grow wild, uncle?"

"Yes, in Africa, where the climate is much warmer than ours; but it cannot stand the cold of our winters. One hard frost kills it."

"Then the fields must be planted every year?"

"Yes, every year, in March or April, seeds are planted. In a week or ten days the plants show themselves.

"By the last of June they begin to bloom. In the morning, when the blooms open, they are of a light cream color; later in the day they change to a deep pink. They die and fall off the second day. Then the bolls begin to form; they grow very fast, and become as large as a small egg.

"When the seeds are ripe, the hot sun bursts the bolls open and shows the beautiful, snow-white cotton within. Then, as you now see, the picking goes on. The fields are alive with workers. After it is picked, the cotton must be ginned and packed into bales.

"You have seen great wagons piled high with such bales. If the cotton were put loosely into sacks, it would take up a great deal of room because it is so fluffy. For this reason, it is squeezed in a great press.

"That strange-looking thing that you see at the end of the gin-house, with two long arms, is the press. There the cotton is pressed and baled. But for sending far away it is best to have the bales still smaller.

"So, in some of the large cities there are more powerful presses than we have on our plantations, and in them the bales are pressed and made a great deal smaller. You shall go to Savannah next week and see one of these 'compresses', as they are called, at work."

"What becomes of all the cotton, uncle?"

"A great deal of it goes to other countries, but much is used in the United States. In the cotton-mills it is cleaned and spun into threads. The threads are woven into cloth, and the cloth is cut up and made into clothes and other useful articles.

"Some years ago a great cotton exhibition was held in Atlanta. All the machines for ginning, spinning, and weaving cotton into cloth were shown in one building In a field nearby, the cotton itself was growing.

"One morning some of this cotton was picked in the field and carried to the hall, where it was twisted into thread, woven into cloth, and made into suits, which were presented to some gentlemen, and worn by them on the evening of the same day."

译文

棉花（2）

"这么大一片棉花地一定有很多很多棉花籽吧，叔叔，要怎么处理它们呢？"

"最好的留着明年种，其他的大多都卖给磨油坊了。在那儿，它们会被拿来榨油。

"压榨器里留有渣滓结成的硬块，可以拿去磨碎后喂养牲口，或给棉花地施肥。"

"棉花籽油是最具价值的商品之一呢。"

"棉树会一直疯长吗，叔叔？"

"会的，在非洲就会，那里的气候比我们这儿要温暖得多。但在我们这儿，棉树没法熬过寒冷的冬天，光是严霜就能把它冻死。"

"所以每年都要开拓田地？"

"是啊，每年都要，在三月或是四月的时候播种。一周或十天内，植物就会长出来了。

"六月前它就开始开花了。清晨刚开的时候，花还是淡黄色，当天晚些时候，就会变成深粉色了。第二天，它们就会凋谢然后掉落。再然后，圆荚就会开始形成；它们长得飞快，会长成一个小鸡蛋那么大。

"等到种子成熟了，圆荚会在烈日下爆开，里面雪白美丽的棉花就会显露出来，然后，就是你所看到的，采摘时节，田地里满是农工。采摘之后，棉花就要被拿去轧棉，然后打包成捆状。

"那些拉着一摞摞堆得高高的棉花捆的大货车，你之前见过。如果把棉花就那样松散地放到麻袋里的话，就会很占地方，因为它们实在是太蓬松了。这样就需要在大型压床下碾轧。

"轧棉房的一头，那个有两只长胳膊的奇怪东西就是压床。棉花就是在那儿被压缩再打包成捆的。然而，为了方便运到很远的地方，捆束越小越好。

"所以在有的大城市里，使用的是比我们的种植园更强力的压床，在那儿棉花被打包、压缩得更小。你下周可以去萨凡纳看看他们口中所说的'绷带'，也就是工作状态的压床。"

"棉花之后要送到哪儿去呢，叔叔？"

"相当多的棉花会被送往其他国家，但大部分还是在美国消耗掉了。在棉花坊里，棉花要洗净，纺成丝线。细线再被织成布料，而后剪裁，然后做成衣服，或者其他有用的东西。

"几年前，亚特兰大在棉花地旁边举办过一个大型棉花展。所有用来轧花、纺纱和编织棉花做成布料的机器都放在同一座大楼里。

"在某一天早晨，他们摘走了这片地里的一些棉花，运到展厅中，缠成线，织成布，做成衣，并展示给在场的先生们，然后，当天晚上这些先生们就能穿上身了。"

Lilies and Cat-Tails(1)

"Mother," said Roger, swinging in at the door, "I am going to begin Physical Geography! And the teacher says that I must have a book, please, as soon as I can get it. It costs two dollars, and it's just full of pictures. May I get it today, please, mother?"

"Mother," looked up with a sad little loving smile,"I have not two dollars in the world just now, unless I take it from the money I am saving to get you a new suit, and I hardly ought to do that, my poor Roger."

With a rueful whistle, Roger looked down at his clothes. They were clean, but were very much patched and darned. "Never mind, mother! Perhaps Will Almy will lend me his book sometimes, or I can study at recess out of Miss Gray's. Don't worry, mother!"

Mrs. Rayne sighed deeply as Roger left the house. She knew that it was to hide his face of disappointment that he ran off in so much haste.

Poor Roger! So eager to learn, he ought to have a first-rate education! But how could she, a poor widow with four children on a tiny farm, give it to him? Bread and butter and clothes must come first, and these were hard enough to win. Education must be picked up as it could.

But Roger, though he was disappointed, had no idea of giving up the Physical Geography. "Mother cannot get it for me," he said,"so I must get it myself. The only question is, how ?"

That evening, just as the sun was setting, a boat pushed out from among the reeds of Pleasant Pond. One boy sat in the center and paddled; another sat in the bow and looked sharply around; while in the stern sat a little girl, who dipped her hands into the water and sang.

"Here's a fine bunch of cat-tails!" cried Roger."Shove her in here, Joe!"

Joe obeyed, and Roger's knife soon cut the stately reeds with their tips of firm, brown velvet.

"Oh, here are the lilies!" cried little Annet. "See, Roger! See how all white and gold! Oh, let me pull them!"

In another moment the boat seemed to be resting on a living carpet of snow and gold. The lilies grew so thick that one could hardly see the water between them.

Roger and Anna drew them in by handfuls, laying them in shining piles in the bottom of the boat.

(Laura E. Richards , adapted)

译文

百合和香蒲(1)

"妈妈,"罗杰大步走进门说,"我想要学自然地理。老师说我必须要先有本课本。自然地理课本里面都是各种图片,需要两美元。妈妈,请问我今天能买课本吗?"

妈妈抬起头,面带一丝忧伤,温和地微笑着说:"我现在真的拿不出两美元。我可怜的罗杰,我本打算给你买件新衣服,省了很久,马上就能凑够钱了。如果要买书,除非从这里面拿出两美元。"

罗杰悲伤地叹了口气,低下头看了看自己的衣服。衣服非常的干净,但却满是补丁。"妈妈,没关系的。也许威尔·艾尔玛可以偶尔把他的课本借给我;我也可以在没有格林老师的情况下,利用休息时间自己学习。妈妈,你别担心!"

看着罗杰离开家,雷恩夫人深深地叹了口气。她知道,罗杰这么快地跑出去,只是为了掩饰他满脸失望而已。

可怜的罗杰!如此渴望学习,他理应接受一流的教育!可是,雷恩夫人是个寡妇,带着四个孩子,她的农场那么小,如何能够满足罗杰的愿望?面包、黄油、衣服才是最要紧的,而且来得也不是那么容易。至于孩子的教育,只能做到哪儿算哪儿了。

虽然罗杰非常的失望,但是他没有放弃学习自然地理的愿望。"妈妈没有办法帮我买课本,"他说,"那么就要靠我自己了。但问题是,我该怎么做呢?"

那天晚上，太阳刚刚下山，一艘小船从满是芦苇的"快乐池塘"驶出来。一个小男孩坐在船桨中间，另一个小男孩坐在船头，仔细地看着周围；在船尾处，还有一个小女孩唱着歌，将自己的手放在水中。

"这儿有一束漂亮的香蒲！"罗杰大声说，"乔，快把船划到这儿。"

乔按照罗杰的话做了，罗杰用刀迅速地砍断水中的芦苇，芦苇的顶端还有一些褐色的穗子绒毛。

"哦，这儿有百合花！"小安纳特叫起来。"看，罗杰，快看！都是白色的，金色的百合花。让我来摘下它们。"

一瞬间，整个船就像是停靠在一张布满白雪和黄金的地毯上。百合花开得密密匝匝，几乎无法看到花朵之间的池塘水面。

罗杰和安纳特一小把一小把地摘着这些百合花，并把闪着光的花朵一束束放在船里。

（劳拉·E.理查兹，有删改）

Lilies and Cat-Tails(2)

The next morning Roger was in the city with the cat-tails and lilies. He looked eagerly about, watching the faces of the passers-by. Would this one buy? Or that one? He held out a bunch timidly, and a lady smiled and stopped.

"How lovely and fresh! Thank you!" and the first piece of silver dropped into Roger's pocket. Soon another followed it, and another, and another, and Roger's hopes rose higher and higher. At this rate the Physical Geography would be his.

His dream was rudely broken in by an old gentleman, who ran against him, nearly knocking him over.

"What! What!" said the gentleman. "Get out of my way, boy!"

"My fault! I beg your pardon!" Roger moved aside, surprised by the sudden shock. "Will you buy some Physical Geographies, sir?" he asked. "See how fresh they are! They are——"

"How dare you talk to me about Physical Geography sir?" said the old gentleman fiercely.

"I——I beg your pardon, sir!" said Roger. "I meant to say 'lilies'. I was thinking so hard about the geography that it slipped out without my knowing it."

"What do you know about Physical Geography?" asked the gentleman.

"Nothing yet, sir," replied Roger modestly. "But I am very anxious to study it. I am selling these lilies and cat-tails to get money enough to buy the book."

"This is a remarkable boy!" cried the old gentleman.

"What geography is it you want? Merton's, I suppose. Trash, sir! trash!"

"No, sir! Willison's," replied the boy, thinking that the old gentleman might be crazy.

But on hearing this, the strange gentleman shook his hand warmly.

"I am Willison!" he exclaimed. "It is my geography! You are a most remarkable boy. I am lad to meet you."

Roger stared blankly. "Did——did you write the Physical Geography?" he stammered.

"To be sure I did," said the gentleman, "and a good job it was! Here! Here!" be cried, feeling in his pockets, "give me the lilies and take that!" and he thrust a shining silver dollar into Roger's hand. "And here," he wrote something on a card, "take that, and go to Cooper, the publisher, and see what he says to you. You are an astonishing boy!"

He was gone, and Roger was sitting on the steps alone.

When he recovered his senses a little, he looked at the card and read in large letters, " Give to the astonishing boy who brings this a copy of my Physical Geography. Best binding. William Willison."

(Laura E. Richards, adapted)

译文

百合花和香蒲（2）

第二天早晨，罗杰带着香蒲和百合花来到市里。他热切地看着来往的行人。这个人会买花吗？这个呢？他小心翼翼地拿出一束花，这时，一位夫人微笑着停下了脚步。

"这花多美，多新鲜啊！谢谢你！"罗杰赚到了卖花的第一份收入。很快另一个人也走了过来，接着第三个人，第四个人，一个接一个的顾客过来。罗杰的愿望实现的机会越来越大。照这样下去，罗杰很快就能买到自然地理书了。

然而，罗杰的愿望很快就被一位老绅士粗暴地打破了。老绅士向罗杰跑来，几乎将罗杰撞倒在地。

"什么情况！"老绅士说，"小伙子，别挡着我的路，给我滚开。这都是你的错！"

"对不起，是我的错。"罗杰被吓了一跳，往旁边挪了挪。

"先生，你想要买一些自然地理书吗？"罗杰问，"看，它们都很新鲜啊！它们……"

"小伙子，你怎么有胆子跟我谈自然地理？"老绅士生气地说。

"先生，我，我，对不起，"罗杰说，"我的意思是百合花多新鲜啊。我一直满脑子想着地理，一不小心就脱口而出了。"

"你都知道哪些自然地理的知识啊？"老绅士问。

"先生，目前为止我什么都不知道。"罗杰谨慎地回答，"但是我非常想学自然地理。我现在在卖这些百合花和香蒲，就是想要凑钱买自然地理书。"

"真是个与众不同的孩子！"老绅士惊叹道，"你想要哪个版本的地理书啊？莫顿版的吗？我认为莫顿版的书一塌糊涂。"

"不是的，先生。我想要威利森版的。"罗杰心想，这个老绅士该不是疯了吧。

听到罗杰这么说，这位陌生的老绅士温和地与罗杰握了握手，解释说："我就是威利森，你想要的书就是我写的。你真是个特别的男孩。很高兴认识你。"

罗杰头脑一片空白，看着绅士，结结巴巴地说："你，你就是自然地理的作者？"

"老实说，我就是，"老绅士回答说，"而且我认为我干得很不错。""对了，"老绅士大声说，并将手伸进了口袋，拿出一个闪亮的银元交到罗杰的手中，"拿着钱，把这朵百合花卖给我。"同时，老绅士还在一张卡片上写了几句话，对罗杰说："拿着这个，去找出版商库珀，看看他会对你说些什么。你真是个特别的孩子！"

老绅士走了，留下罗杰一个人坐在台阶上。罗杰的心情稍微平静一些之后，他打开卡片，看到上面用写着一行大字："给这个带着卡片来的男孩子一本我写的《自然地理》。祝好。威廉姆·威利森。"

（劳拉·E. 理查兹，有删改）

✧ 作者介绍

当理查兹夫人还在波士顿读书时，她就开始为报纸写故事和诗歌。从那时起，她就一直坚持写作。理查兹夫人的家乡在缅因州。

Jack and Tony's Friendship(1)

One bright September morning Jack got out his boat and started for a sail down the river. There was a fresh breeze from the southwest, and as Mrs. Randolph watched him sitting in the stern of the boat with the tiller in his hand, and the big sail swiftly drawing the little shell down the river, she felt a sinking at the heart.

Jack sailed down gaily enough until he got to Lone Point. The sun was shining brightly; but just ahead of him, on the broad bay, was a shadow moving fast across the green water, and turning the waves black.

"That's a squall," said Jack. But he thought that it was not yet time to take down the sail.

Just as he had reached this opinion, the squall struck him. The sail flapped wildly for a moment, and bent lower and lower toward the water.

Suddenly the boat gave a lurch, and Jack soon found himself in the water, drenched to the bone, but clinging to the bottom of the boat, which was driving toward the sandy shore.

Tony Scaife, who had just come in from looking at his nets, was standing in the water, as the boat drifted his way. He waded out as far as he could.

The long tiller rope floated toward him. Tony caught it, and in two minutes Jack was on shore very wet, but otherwise all right.

Tony helped him to haul the boat up, and to take out the sail and spread it on the ground to dry. Then the trouble began.

"Why didn't you take your sail down when you saw the squall coming?" asked Tony.

"Because I wasn't afraid," answered Jack coolly.

"That doesn't mean being afraid," said Tony, with equal coolness. "That's commonsense."

Jack took fire at this.

"You had better mind your business and keep a civil tongue," he snapped.

"I'm civil enough," replied Tony, in a sort of drawl that made Jack angry, "but I thought when I saw you sailing down with that squall just a-humming across the bay, 'That fellow isn't fit to be trusted in a boat by himself.'"

Jack stared at him. He had a high opinion of himself, and no boy had ever before talked to him in that way.

"Look here!" said Jack after a minute, eying Tony hard. "Aren't you a Yankee?"

"Well, I rather guess I am," said Tony.

"Then," said Jack, "you are a rascal, and you know it."

Jack was much larger than Tony, though only a year older, but by the time the words were out of his mouth, Tony was upon him.

Neither wasted any words on the matter, and presently they were rolling over on the sand together, fighting as hard as they could.

Tony showed a good deal of strength, but Jack was too much for him. It took about five minutes for Tony to be really whipped.

But although Tony had been beaten, his spirit was unbroken, and he was as plucky in defeat as in victory—which, after all, is the only real courage.

"Now," said Jack, breathing very fast and folding his arms, "don't you dare to speak to me or to look at me, you rascal."

"I'm no rascal," gasped Tony, looking Jack straight in the eye, "you're bigger than I am, that's all; but if you had been my size, I'd have given you the worst whipping you ever had."

At this, Jack jumped at him. But Tony was too quick. With a sudden jerk he laid Jack sprawling on the sand, and was well out of the way before Jack could get up.

(Molly Elliot Seawell, adapted)

译义

杰克与托尼的友谊（1）

　　九月的一天清晨，天气晴朗，杰克坐上他的小船，扬帆起航，顺流而下。一阵清风从西南面徐徐吹来，杰克坐在船尾，手里拿着舵柄，小船鼓起巨大的风帆，以飞快的速度沿河而下，而伦道夫太太此时正在一旁观望，心情低落。

　　在到达孤独角之前，杰克一路上都是兴高采烈的。这是一片宽阔的港湾，即便当时阳光灿烂，但杰克眼前却出现了一道影子，它快速地掠过碧绿的水域，把浪潮变成了黑色。

　　"那是一阵暴风。"杰克说道。但他认为，现在还不是拆掉风帆的时候。

　　杰克刚想到这一点，暴风便向他袭来。风帆猛烈地拍打了一阵子，就越来越靠近水面。

　　突然，船身一斜，杰克瞬间就落入了水中，浑身都湿透了。但他紧紧抓住了船底，朝着沙滩漂去。

　　托尼·斯凯夫正站在水中，盯着他的渔网。就在这时，漂浮的小船出现在了他的视线里，于是他艰难地走向那只小船，尽量靠近它。

　　系在舵柄上的绳子向托尼漂来，被他一把抓住。两分钟后，杰克被救上岸边，全身都湿透了，但并无大碍。

　　托尼帮忙把小船拖上岸，又把风帆取出，摊在地面上晾晒。然后，托尼与杰克之间有了麻烦。

　　"为什么你看到了暴风还不去取下风帆呢？"托尼问道。

　　"因为我不害怕。"杰克冷静地回答。

　　"这不是害不害怕的问题，"托尼同样冷静地说道，"这是常识。"

　　这句话激怒了杰克。

　　"你最好别多管闲事，讲话礼貌点。"杰克生气地说道。

　　"我很礼貌，"托尼回答，他故意拖长声调，这让杰克更为恼怒，"但是当我看到你仍然扬帆在暴风中前行时，我仿佛听见，港湾上传来一阵"嗡嗡"的声响，说'在船上的那个家伙，真不该相信自己啊'。"

杰克两眼瞪着托尼，他对自己很有自信，而且以前也从来没有人那样对他说话。

"听着！"杰克一分钟后说道，以犀利的目光望向托尼，"你不就是个美国佬吗？"

"嗯，我宁可是美国佬。"托尼说。

"所以，"杰克说道，"你也知道的，你就是个流氓。"

尽管杰克仅仅比托尼年长一岁，却比托尼的个头大得多。但是，这样的话语从杰克嘴里一出，托尼便占了上风。

他们不再浪费口舌，两人立刻在沙滩上翻滚着，激烈地厮打起来。

虽然托尼也使出了浑身解数，但杰克还是比他厉害得多。五分钟后，托尼彻底输了。

尽管托尼被打败了，但他的气势尚在，不管成败与否，他都不屈不挠，毕竟这才是一个真正有勇气的人。

"现在，"杰克气喘吁吁地说道，双臂交叉放在胸前，"你这个流氓，还敢和我说话吗？还敢直视我的眼睛吗？"

"我不是流氓，"托尼上气不接下气地说道，两人四目相对，"你能打赢我，只是因为你的身材比较高大而已；但如果你和我的身材一样，那我一定可以给你最惨痛的教训。"

听到这儿，杰克扑向托尼，但托尼太敏捷了，他猛地一拽，将杰克拉倒了。杰克趴在沙滩上，一点都使不上劲，过了一会儿才站起来。

（莫莉·埃利奥特·西韦尔，有删改）

Jack and Tony's Friendship(2)

It was about two o'clock when Jack's boat was tied up at the Marrowbone Wharf. Jack came swaggering up to the house to tell his adventures to his mother.

Mrs. Randolph was sitting on the broad porch, where the overhanging branches of the elms and big live-oaks made a flickering shade. She heard Jack through without a word. Then she said very quietly:

"So after the boy had helped you with the boat and the sail, you called him a rascal for telling you the truth?"

"Y——yes I was," answered Jack, rather surprised at the new way his mother put it.

"And then you whipped him, although you were twice as big as he?"

"Then,"said Mrs. Randolph, rising, "go upstairs at once, change your clothes, and walk down to Lone Point. Ask for Tony, and make him the very best apology you can for your unmanly conduct. Go into the cottage then, and ask his mother's pardon for fighting on her land; and when you come home, I shall have something further to say to you."

Jack looked at his mother in surprise. There was no trifling with her; besides, it came home to him how mean his conduct had been.

Without a word he went to his room, and came back within ten minutes. He went up to his mother, looking very pale.

"Mother," he said, "you are right. I was the rascal, not Tony. I promise you I'll never, as long as I live, do such a thing again."

His mother said nothing. She was not often displeased with him; but when she was, she did not quickly relent.

Jack set off with a weight of shame upon his heart.

He was a Virginia gentleman! He felt like a coward and everything else that was mean.

When he reached Lone Point, he found Tony sitting on the little porch, mending his nets, while his mother sewed on a ragged sail.

Tony was very silent. He felt keenly how he had been treated, and being a very human sort of boy, he longed to be large enough to fight Jack Randolph and whip him.

When Jack reached the step, he took off his hat and, without knowing it, put on his best manner.

"How do you do, madam?" he said. "I believe that you are Mrs. Scaife."

The widow rose quickly.

"Yes," she said. "I'm Mrs. Scaife."

"And I am Jack Randolph," continued Jack, still keeping his head uncovered. "I came to ask your pardon for fighting on your land today. I know that it was very ungentlemanly. I feel very bad about it, and so does my mother, and I hope you'll overlook it."

Then Jack turned to Tony, who had stopped mending his nets, and was looking very hard before him.

"I do not know what to say to you," said Jack. "You helped me with the boat and the sail, and you didn't say or do anything, and I'm bigger than you, and I behaved like a bully——and a coward, and I'm ashamed of myself. I came here to tell you so, and to ask you to shake hands and overlook it."

A queer look came into Tony's blue eyes.

"I don't think that you are a coward. I think you're a pretty brave fellow," he said. Then the two boys shook hands.

The Widow Scaife's eyes filled with tears.

"I thought hard of you before you came," she said, "but now I think that you're a real man, and I forgive you. I hope Tony will."

"Yes," said Tony," and if you'll come down here some morning, we'll go fishing together."

The two boys began to talk about fishing then, and got on very well.

As Jack and Tony were sturdy and excellent fellows in their way, it is not strange that they soon became the closest friends. Jack found thorough manliness and independence in Tony, who had taken upon himself the balance of the payment for the few acres at Lone Point and worked and contrived to that end.

Tony for the first time associated with a boy higher bred and carefully brought up. Their very differences drew them together, and the two boys without knowing it at all, helped each other to become better men.

(Molly Elliot Seawell, adapted)

译文

杰克与托尼的友谊（2）

大概在两点钟的时候，杰克的船停靠在"髓骨"码头。他大摇大摆地回到家里，告诉母亲今天的遭遇。

宽敞的走廊里悬挂着榆树和常青橡树的枝条。橡树的枝条很粗，倒映的影子忽隐忽现。伦道夫太太就坐在走廊，她就听着杰克说他的经历，一言不发。然后，她轻声说道：

"所以，在这个男孩帮你弄好小船和风帆之后，因为他说了实话，你就叫他流氓吗？"

"是……是的。"杰克回答，他没想到，母亲会从这个角度看这件事。

"然后你就把他打倒，尽管你的个头是他的一倍？"

"那么，"伦道夫太太站起来说道："你立刻上楼，换一套衣服，再去一次孤独角。你要找到托尼，为你毫无男子气概的行为，向他致以最深的歉意。然后再去托尼的家里，找到他的母亲，求她原谅你在她的地盘打架；等你回家之后，我还有一些话要对你说。"

杰克不解地看着母亲。母亲非常严肃；回到家之后他才知道自己的品行有多么恶劣。

杰克二话不说，马上跑回房间，十分钟后就出来了。他去到母亲跟前，只见母亲气得脸色苍白。

"妈妈，"他说，"你说得对。托尼不是流氓，我才是。我向您保证，我这辈子再也不会做这种事情了。"

母亲什么也没说。她不经常对杰克发火，但一旦发火，就不会轻易心软。

杰克无比羞愧地出发了。

杰克是弗吉尼亚州的绅士！而今他觉得自己就是一个懦夫，其他的一切都微不足道。

杰克来到了孤独角，他看到托尼坐在窄小的走廊里，修补他的渔网，而他的母亲正在缝补一张破旧的风帆。

托尼是个非常安静的人。但他还记得两人之间的龃龉，而且作为一个男孩子，他骨子里也很渴望拥有强健的体魄，可以狠狠地把杰克·伦道夫击倒在地。

当杰克来到台阶前时，他脱下了帽子。虽然他不懂礼节，但他尽力做到最好。

"您好，女士。"他说，"想必您就是斯凯夫太太。"

这位寡妇迅速地站了起来。

"是的，"她说，"我就是斯凯夫太太。"

"我是杰克·伦道夫，"杰克继续说道，一直没戴上自己的帽子，"我是来乞求您的宽恕的，我今天在你的地盘上打架了。我知道这样的行为很没有教养，我和我的母亲为此感到十分惭愧。我希望您能原谅我。"

接着，杰克转向托尼。托尼放下手中的活，怒气冲冲地看向杰克。

"我不知道该和你说什么，"杰克说道，"你帮我拉小船上岸，帮我整理风帆，你没骂过我，也没打过我，而且你的个头比较小，我却横行霸道。我其实就是一个懦夫，我为自己感到羞愧。我来这里就想告诉你这些，然后希望能和你握握手，请求你的原谅。"

这时，托尼的眼睛里露出了惊异的神色。

"我不认为你是个懦夫。我认为你是个非常勇敢的小伙子。"他说。然后，这两个男孩便握手言和了。

斯凯夫太太热泪盈眶。

"在你来之前，我对你的印象很不好，"她说，"但是现在，你是一个真正的男子汉，我原谅你了，我希望托尼也可以原谅你。"

"是的，"托尼说，"如果以后有机会，你可以早上来这里，我们一起去钓鱼。"

于是，这两个男孩就讲起钓鱼的事情来了，他们相处得十分融洽。

杰克和托尼都很勇敢、很优秀，他们很快就成了最亲密的伙伴，这一点也不稀奇。杰克发现，托尼是个刚毅、独立的人。托尼努力地工作，负担了自己在孤独角的开销。

这是托尼第一次交到杰克这样的朋友——体格比他强壮，从小娇生惯养。但是，正是他们之间的不同点让他们走到了一起，他们根本不介意这些不同，而是互相帮助，共同进步。

（莫莉·埃利奥特·西韦尔，有删改）

作者介绍

1880年，西韦尔的文章《小贾维斯》荣获由"青春伴侣"颁发的500美金的奖励。从那时候开始，她创作了大量出色的作品，大多数和海军有关，例如《保罗·琼斯》《迪凯特与萨默斯》和《十二位船长》。杰克与托尼的故事出自《同甘共苦》一书，本文转载已征得洛斯罗普出版社、李与谢泼德出版公司的许可。

练习

1. 抄写

(1) The horns of the ram → The ram's horns.

(2) The shoes of Timothy → Timothy's shoes.

2. 仿照上面的例子改写句子。

(1) The best friend of Raleigh.

(2) The kingdom of Jason.

(3) The father of Peter.

(4) The chicken of the Blue Hen.

(5) The nest of an oriole.

(6) The mother of Jack Randolph.

Rosetta Pope's School

"What are you doing?"

It was Rosetta's uncle that asked the question. Rosetta looked up with a little laugh.

"I'm playing school," she said.

Uncle Leonard came near and gazed at her row of pupils, first in wonder, then with an amused smile.

"You have some very famous scholars," he observed.

A dozen or more "Author" cards were ranged on chairs before her, and each card pictured the face of a man or a woman well known in literature.

"Is Tennyson at the head or the foot of the class?" Uncle Leonard asked, his eyes twinkling.

"Oh, at the head!" Rosetta answered. "I don't know what other people think, but I rank them first just as I like them, and then if they don't recite well, they have to go down."

"Pray, what do they recite?" her uncle asked. "Spelling and geography?"

"Of course not! They recite from their own work——here are the lessons," and she laid her hand on a big pile of books at her right.

"Do you admit visitors?"

"Oh, yes! Mamma often comes in. That's the visitor's seat," she pointing to a great arm-chair.

So from the other side of the room Uncle Leonard watched the small teacher and her famous scholars.

"Lord Tennyson will please recite his New Year's poem, beginning: 'Ring out, wild bells, to the wild sky.' "

Then Rosetta selected a book from the pile, and keeping her finger in the place, recited the lines with very little hesitation.

"Well done!" praised her uncle.

"Thank you," said Rosetta.

The next card bore the face of Alexander Pope, and the teacher said,

"Mr. Pope, you may recite two lines from your 'Essay on Man'." Again Rosetta spoke for her pupil:

"Honor and shame from no condition rise;
Act well thy part, there all the honor lies."

"I don't understand much of his work," she exclaimed, "but as our names are the same, I thought that I should put him in somewhere, and he has learned those lines so well that he stays up near the head."

Uncle Leonard burst out laughing, but was checked by Rosetta's warning finger.

"Mr. Cowper, please give us the first and last stanzas of John Gilpin."

Rosetta began bravely enough:

"John Gilpin was a citizen
Of credit and renown;
A——"

Silently she puckered her forehead, and then said in a voice supposed to be stern,

"Mr. Cowper, you may go to the foot!" Adding to her uncle, "I never can remember that, but I like it."

"And how often do you have this sort of thing?" asked Uncle Leonard.

"Oh, whenever I get lonesome. I would rather have you talk to me now," and with a sweep of her hand, she gathered her famous pupils into a pack, and tossed it on the table.

"Tell me about Cousin Maud, please!" she coaxed.

"One thing about her is that she is lonely most of the time, as we live so far from neighbors. I think that I shall buy her a set of 'Authors' on my way home, and tell her about this school of yours."

"Oh, do!" cried Rosetta. "And then when she comes down here next summer, we can play school together. Mamma likes it, because she says it teaches me so much."

"I should say so! I shall have to coach Maud first; she doesn't know one author from another."

"Neither did I until I learned," said Rosetta.

(Emma C. Dowd)

译文

罗塞塔·蒲柏的学校

"你在干什么呢?"

罗塞塔的叔叔问她。罗塞塔抬头给了他一个浅浅的笑容。

"我在玩教学游戏呢。"她说。

莱纳德叔叔走到她身边,盯着她的一排学生看,刚开始有点惊讶,然后被逗笑了。

他观察了一会儿,说:"你有一些非常有名的学生呢。"

她前面排列着一打(也可能更多)"作家"卡片,每张卡片上都画着一张男人或是女人的脸,他们都是知名的文学家。

莱纳德叔叔眼睛闪闪发光,问她:"丁尼生是班里的第一名还是最后一名?"

"哦,他是第一名!"罗塞塔回答,"我不知道其他人是怎么想的,但是我是按照我对他们的喜爱程度排列卡片的。此外,如果他们背得不好,就得降一名。"

"那请问他们要背诵什么呢?"她的叔叔问道,"拼写和地理?"

"当然不是!他们背诵他们自己的作品——功课在这里。"她把手放在右边的一大堆书上。

"你允许有人旁听吗?"

"哦,允许!妈妈经常走进来。那里是旁听者的座位。"她一边说,一边指着一个很大的扶手椅。

于是莱纳德叔叔坐进扶手椅,在房间的另一头看着这位小老师和她的那些著名的学生。

"丁尼生大人会很高兴背诵他的新年诗,这就开始了,'敲响了,狂野的钟声,向着无垠的天空。'"

罗塞塔从书堆里挑了一本书,用手指点着,毫不犹豫地背诵起诗行。

"干得好!"她的叔叔赞扬道。

"谢谢你。"罗塞塔说。

接下来的一张卡片上画着亚历山大·蒲柏的脸，于是小老师说："蒲柏先生，你要背诵你的《论人》当中的两行。"罗塞塔再次为她的学生背诵：

"荣誉和羞耻的产生没有条件。你的表现良好，荣誉就会产生。"

"我不太能理解这句话。"她宣布说，"但是我们同姓，我想我应该给他安排个位置，而且他学得很好，一直名列前茅。"

莱纳德叔叔爆发出一阵大笑，但立即被罗塞塔警告的手势阻止了。

"库珀先生，请你给我们背诵《约翰·吉尔平》的第一小节和最后一小节。"

罗塞塔很勇敢地开始了：

"公民约翰·吉尔平德高望重；一个——"

她无声地皱起了额头，然后用一种听上去很严厉的声音说：

"库珀先生，你可能会变成最后一名！"

她又对她的叔叔说："我从来都记不住这一首，但是我很喜欢它。"

莱纳德叔叔问她："你多久玩一次这样的游戏？"

她挥了一下手，说："哦，每当我孤单一人的时候就会玩这个游戏，不过现在我更喜欢你跟我说话。"她把她那些著名的学生聚拢成一小堆，然后把他们扔在台子上。

"请你跟我说说莫德堂姐吧！"她撒娇地要求道。

"我们和邻居住得很远，所以大部分时间她很孤单。我想我在回家的路上应该给她买一套'作家'卡片，然后把你办的学校讲给她听。"

"哦，就这么干吧！"罗塞塔喊道，"等她下个暑假来这里的时候，我们可以一起玩学校游戏。妈妈喜欢这个游戏，因为她说它教会了我很多东西。"

"我完全同意！我得先培训一下莫德；她不知道这么多的作家。"

罗塞塔说："我学会之前也不知道。"

（艾玛·C.多德）

《美国语文》译者名录

钱志慧	南京师范大学
帕孜丽娅	暨南大学
尹吴娅琪	中南财经政法大学
侯艺东	南京师范大学
夏婕	南方医科大学
金晓寒	复旦大学
张佳佳	南京林业大学
杜子悦	华中师范大学
高倩	华东师范大学
蒋荟蓉	西南交通大学
赵艺珂	南开大学
苌婧	四川外国语大学
李颖	北京外国语大学

美工

彭慧	华东师范大学